PENGUIN

THE SYMPO

PLATO (*c.* 427–347 BC) stands with Socrates and Aristotle as one of the founders of the Western intellectual tradition. He came from a family that had long played a prominent part in Athenian politics, and it would have been natural for him to follow the same course. He declined to do so, however, disgusted by the violence and corruption of Athenian political life, and sickened especially by the execution in 399 of his friend and teacher, Socrates. Inspired by Socrates' inquiries into the nature of ethical standards, Plato sought a cure for the ills of society not in politics but in philosophy, and arrived at the conclusion that those ills would not cease until philosophers became rulers or rulers philosophers. At an uncertain date in the early fourth century BC he founded in Athens the Academy, the first permanent institution devoted to philosophical research and teaching, and the prototype of all Western universities. He travelled extensively, notably to Sicily as political adviser to Dionysius II, ruler of Syracuse.

Plato wrote over twenty philosophical dialogues, and there are also extant under his name thirteen letters, whose genuineness is keenly disputed. His literary activity extended over perhaps half a century: few other writers have exploited so effectively the grace, precision, flexibility and power of Greek prose.

CHRISTOPHER JOHN GILL was born in Cornwall in 1946 and was educated at Cowbridge Grammar School, St John's College, Cambridge, and Yale University. He has taught at the universities of Yale and Bristol, and the University of Wales, Aberystwyth, and is now Professor of Ancient Thought at the University of Exeter. He held a one-year research fellowship at the National Humanities Center, North Carolina, USA. He has written widely on ancient philosophy and literature, his special interests being Plato's use of dialogue form and conceptions of self. His books include a commentary on Plato's Atlantis story, a survey of Greek thought, and *Personality in Greek Epic, Tragedy, and Philosophy: The Self in Dialogue* (1996). He has also edited or co-edited volumes on concepts of personhood, ancient ideas of fiction, form and argument in late Plato, passions in Roman thought, and reciprocity in ancient Greece. He enjoys walking on Dartmoor and swimming on the Cornish coast with friends and his wife and four sons.

PLATO

THE SYMPOSIUM

Translated with an introduction and notes by
CHRISTOPHER GILL

PENGUIN BOOKS

PENGUIN BOOKS

Published by the Penguin Group
Penguin Books Ltd, 80 Strand, London WC2R ORL, England
Penguin Putnam Inc., 375 Hudson Street, New York, New York 10014, USA
Penguin Books Australia Ltd, 250 Camberwell Road, Camberwell, Victoria 3124, Australia
Penguin Books Canada Ltd, 10 Alcorn Avenue, Toronto, Ontario, Canada M4V 3B2
Penguin Books India (P) Ltd, 11 Community Centre,
Panchsheel Park, New Delhi – 110 017, India
Penguin Books (NZ) Ltd, Cnr Rosedale and Airborne Roads,
Albany, Auckland, New Zealand
Penguin Books (South Africa) (Pty) Ltd, 24 Sturdee Avenue, Rosebank 2196, South Africa

Penguin Books Ltd, Registered Offices: 80 Strand, London WC2R ORL, England

www.penguin.com

Published in Penguin Classics 1999
Reprinted 200

040

Copyright © Christopher Gill, 1999
All rights reserved

The moral right of the translator and editor has been asserted

Set in 10/13 pt PostScript Monotype Bembo
Typeset by Rowland Phototypesetting Ltd, Bury St Edmunds, Suffolk
Printed and bound in Great Britain by Clays Ltd, Elcograf S.p.A.

ISBN-13: 978-0-140-44927-3

www.greenpenguin.co.uk

CONTENTS

PREFACE

Walter Hamilton's Penguin translation of Plato's *Symposium* has, for nearly fifty years, successfully introduced many readers – including me – to this fascinating work. However, Hamilton's English has become rather dated. Also it is now normal for Penguin translations, like others, to provide more scholarly help to the reader, through introduction and notes, than was expected when Hamilton produced his edition. So I was happy to accept Penguin's invitation to prepare a new edition. In the translation, I have aimed at being as accurate as possible, while also trying to find a modern English equivalent for Plato's lucid and flexible Greek prose. The *Symposium* presents the additional challenge of differently characterized styles of speech and of subtle interplay between the philosophical ideas and the narrative or dramatic context. I have not systematically reproduced Plato's sentence-structure. His frequent use of long and syntactically complex sentences is out of key with modern English prose. Also I have not necessarily translated any given Greek word by a single English equivalent. I recognize that, in Plato's more technical or dialectical passages, it is important to use one-word equivalents; and in the more dialectical parts of the *Symposium* (in Socrates' argument with Agathon and Diotima's speech) I have done this. For instance, in such passages, the Greek word *kalos* is uniformly translated as 'beautiful'. But in other contexts I have translated it as 'attractive, good-looking' or 'fine, right', as the context seems to require, in a way that reflects the non-technical character of the discourse in this Platonic dialogue. The translation is based throughout on the text of Kenneth Dover's edition (*Plato: Symposium*, Cambridge, 1980). Dover's commentary is outstandingly clear and helpful for those wishing to read the dialogue in Greek.

Like Hamilton, I have provided a full introduction, which examines the content and significance of the speeches as well as setting the *Symposium* in its social and intellectual context. There are also short notes to the translation, giving relevant background information and guidance on the structure and presentation of the discussion. By contrast with most other Penguin editions of Plato, the translation itself is not punctuated by comment and analysis. The *Symposium* is relatively straightforward and readable; it also has a clear literary as well as philosophical unity. So it seemed better to leave the translation to stand on its own. Readers may choose to read the translation through first, and then turn to the Introduction as a way of exploring issues raised by the text. The Introduction serves in turn as a gateway to the many interesting recent discussions of the *Symposium* listed in the Select Bibliography.

I am grateful to Robin Waterfield (then an adviser for Penguin Classics) for suggesting that I prepare this new translation, and also for the excellent example he has given in his own World's Classics edition of this text. I would like to thank Christopher Rowe for giving me a copy of the stimulating lectures which form the basis of his own Aris and Phillips edition; also to Frisbee Sheffield for sending me her suggestive paper on philosophical creativity in Plato. My colleague John Wilkins kindly found time to make valuable comments on my translation and introduction. I have learnt much from the successive generations of students with whom I have studied the *Symposium* in Greek or in translation. I am most grateful to the Penguin Classics editors, Paul Keegan and Anna South, for their great patience in waiting for me to find time to complete this edition, and hope that the end-product justifies their patience. Thanks are due also to Monica Schmoller for her perceptive and careful copy-editing.

Note on Conventions

All unidentified references in the Introduction and Notes are to the *Symposium* (abbreviated as *Symp.*). References are to the standard Stephanus page numbers and letters in the outer margin of the page. Modern scholarly books and articles are cited by author and date alone; full references are given in the Select Bibliography at the end of this volume.

Christopher Gill
Exeter

INTRODUCTION

Plato's *Symposium* is one of the most striking and famous studies of love in Western thought. It is both a powerful philosophical examination of love and a great work of literature, in which the dramatic representation of characters reinforces intellectual speech-making and argument. Together with Plato's other works on this topic (*Lysis* and *Phaedrus*), the *Symposium* has been immensely influential on thinking about love from antiquity to the present day, especially in the Italian Renaissance.[1] It offers us a special insight into two central features of social life in Classical Greece: the formal drinking-party and homosexuality or homo-eroticism. Although it reflects its specific historical situation, the *Symposium* is highly accessible to modern readers. It raises questions about love that are absolutely fundamental; the most important speech, that of Socrates, serves as a challenge to the unexamined romanticism of much modern thinking.

Is the *Symposium* about love – or desire? Plato's dialogue centres on a series of speeches praising *erôs*, a term usually translated 'desire'. One of the meanings of *erôs* is 'passionate sexual desire'; and it is also the name of one of the two Greek gods of love, Eros (in Latin, Cupid). But some of the speeches, especially Socrates', suggest that sexual desire is an expression of certain deeper and more universal types of desire or motivation. The speeches also link *erôs* with the kind of affectionate concern that forms part of close relationships between family-members or friends. The normal Greek term for this concern is *philia*, often translated as 'friendship'. So, taken as a whole, *erôs* in the *Symposium* has the same broad range of meanings as 'love', and is usually translated in that way in this translation. Most of the speeches are about the kind of 'love' that modern readers can easily recognize as that, located in emotionally charged relationships between individual people. However, as noted, Socrates places *erôs* in a much broader framework; and one of the key questions raised by the *Symposium* is whether Socrates' speech is about interpersonal love or about human desire and motivation in general.

The Symposium in Greek Life

Plato's dialogue represents a symposium: what is this? Though this can be translated, rather inadequately, as 'drinks-party', it is closer to a modern private dinner-party. But there are important differences between a Greek symposium and modern dinner-party. These reflect the male-dominated character of Greek social life, and the relative segregation of male and female activities. They also reflect the ritualization of social life, even in what we see as areas of privacy or informality. For one thing, the host and guests were all men; the symposium took place in the *andrôn*, the main room in the men's part of the house. In Archaic Greece (seventh–sixth century BC), the symposium seems to have served as an important context of male bonding between aristocrats, the dominant group in Greek states at that time. Aristocratic young men and boys took part as cupbearers and observers, and received both ethical advice and homo-erotic attention; in these ways they were initiated into adult male social life.[2]

In late fifth-century Athens, where Plato's dialogue is set, the symposium remained a largely aristocratic pastime, though Athens was by then a democracy. The participants were now adult males; free-born boys no longer took part, and their place was taken by male and female slaves who provided service and entertainment. By contrast with the modern dinner-party, there was a clear separation between the meal and the subsequent drinking, and the drinking was more fully ritualized. After the meal was cleared away, the guests had their hands washed, and were sometimes garlanded with flowers and anointed with perfumed oils. The symposium began with a taste of unmixed wine, poured out in honour of 'the good spirit' (*daimôn*), and accompanied by hymns to the god. Subsequently, wine was mixed with water in a bowl (*kratêr*), normally in the proportion of five parts water to two of wine; the resulting drink was comparable in strength with modern beer. One person (the 'symposiarch') was elected to set, in consultation with others, the precise strength of the wine mixture, the number of bowls to be mixed (three was a standard number), and the size of cups to be used.

The *andrôn* was a square room, with a raised floor on all sides, on which were arranged, typically, between seven and eleven couches. Guests reclined on the couches, usually two to a couch, leaning on cushions with their left elbows, leaving their right hands free to eat and drink from low tables in front of them. The couches formed a square, broken by the door; the first position (in front of the door) seems to have been most favoured, perhaps as the first to be served food, and the last least so. This arrangement promoted reciprocal conversation or song around and across the square. Wine and 'taking turns' in song or speech went round the room, usually from left to right. The windowless room often had wall-paintings; the scenes, like those on the decorated mixing-bowl and cups, might be those of symposia or erotic encounters. The whole context created a sealed and privileged space, in which the attention of the guests was focused on each other and on their shared enjoyment of wine, talk, music and sensuality. Erotic company was provided by female (slave) courtesans and sometimes their male equivalents, who served as musical entertainers and 'escorts'; their erotic role at the symposium seems to have been more or less explicit flirtation rather than sexual intercourse, which might have occurred later.[3]

Plato's symposium is in many ways typical of this social practice, for which it provides useful evidence. But the director of Plato's symposium, Eryximachus, conspicuously sends away the female entertainer provided by Agathon, their host. This signals the unusually intellectual character of this symposium, with its series of speeches on the nature of love; it also paves the way for a focus on homo-erotic love. The intensely philosophical mood created by Socrates' speech is shattered by the entry of the drunken Alcibiades and a group of revellers, including a (courtesan) flute-girl. Alcibiades breaks the normal sympotic conventions by electing himself symposi-arch, by drinking wine neat and making others do the same. He is subsequently incorporated into the more civilized arrangements of their group; but he breaks their conventions again by giving a eulogy of Socrates, instead of the god of love, and by frank talk about sex between the two of them – though this turns out to be frank talk about the *absence* of sex.

Homo-eroticism

Parties were important to drink wine and mingle to get to know each other. This was a comm greek practice

A marked feature of the *Symposium*, as of other early and middle Platonic dialogues, is the emphasis on sexual (or at least erotic) relations between males. How far is this typical of the symposium, or of Athenian life at this time? How far is it peculiar to the Socratic circle, as Plato presents this?

Modern scholarship, especially that of Kenneth Dover and Michel Foucault, has done much to locate this feature within the larger pattern of Greek sexual practices and attitudes, as far as we can reconstruct these. It is now accepted that 'homosexuality' is a modern, post-Freudian category. In ancient Greek culture, as in some others, there is a widespread assumption that male sexual and erotic desire may be directed, in a non-exclusive way, at males as well as females. A familiar pattern in Greek culture in the Archaic (seventh–sixth century BC) and Classical (fifth–fourth century BC) periods is that in which an adult male is attracted to a boy or young man, especially when the latter is between puberty and growing a beard (which marked the entry into full manhood). Scholars usually see this relationship as an asymmetrical one: the older partner (the lover) takes the initiative and gains greater sexual pleasure; the younger (the boyfriend or loved one) gains the friendship and help of the older man. (This is one example of what is often seen as a more general feature of Greek thought about sexuality: the clear distinction between 'the lover' and the 'loved one' or between the 'active' and 'passive' sexual roles.)[4] The relationship may belong to a phase, or an aspect, of the life of the older or younger man; the lover may be married to a woman at the time, or he (like the boyfriend) may do so later. Lifelong, exclusive male couples, such as Pausanias and Agathon in the *Symposium*,[5] are exceptional. Although this seems to have been a relatively familiar social pattern, it was (as Foucault stresses) a potentially problematic one, especially when both partners were free, citizen males. In particular, the boyfriend had to avoid over-ready compliance and to be careful about accepting money or favours; this could leave him open to the charge of being a prostitute and so lead to loss of citizen-rights.[6]

Against the background of these attitudes, the ready acceptance of homo-erotic attraction in the *Symposium* is less surprising. However, we should not see the dialogue as wholly representative of its culture in this respect. As James Davidson stresses, in a recent book on sensuality in Classical Athens, most evidence points to a predominantly heterosexual society, in which male sexual activity was largely centred on wives or (female) prostitutes or courtesans.[7] The great gap in Classical Athens, from a modern standpoint, is the failure to romanticize male–female courtship and subsequent marriage. Various factors explain this, including the early age at which girls married (around fourteen), their rigid seclusion from men prior to this, and the separation of male and female roles within marriage. As a result, 'romantic love' in Classical Greece (and, to an extent, in later antiquity) tends to be focused on relations between free adult males and courtesans or (less frequently) their male equivalents.[8] A further area of 'romantic' sexuality, already noted, is that between males of citizen status, especially between an older and a younger man. The emphasis in the *Symposium* on this type of eroticism is thus not wholly typical of the culture, though it may reflect attitudes and practices in some aristocratic circles, especially intellectual ones.[9]

There is a particular feature in Athenian life which promotes eroticism between citizen males, while at the same time making it problematic. It is also one that the *Symposium* helps to bring out. In Classical Athens, and in Greece generally, high-status activities such as athletics, warfare, politics, philosophy and rhetoric were exclusive to free males. Although the value of distinctive female activities was sometimes recognized, Greek conceptions of 'virtue' and 'happiness' centred on these high-status male activities. This gave a special importance to erotic relations between those eligible to participate in such activities. Several of the speeches in the *Symposium* centre on the connection between eroticism and 'virtue'; and the type of virtue involved is predominantly that linked with these activities.[10] The *Symposium*, together with some other Platonic and non-Platonic evidence for this period, gives special prominence to what we can call the 'erotic-educational' relationship. This is one between an older and a younger male, in which the older initiates the younger into 'virtue', as understood in male citizen circles. Pausanias' speech presents this type of relationship as an ideal form of love; Socrates, speaking as Diotima, idealizes a modified (non-sexual, philosophical) form of this relationship.[11] This seems to be an important social and sexual pattern in the intellectual, aristocratic circles represented in the Platonic dialogues, though it is one towards which Plato's Socrates has a complex, ambiguous relationship, discussed later (xxxvi–xxxix).

Speech was important to define sexual practice.

Plato and the Dialogue Form

Where does the *Symposium* fit in Plato's writings and thought? All the philosophical writings of Plato (*c*. 427–347 BC) take the form of dialogues. Although little is known for certain about Plato's aims as an author or the exact chronology of the dialogues, some general points can be made. Plato's dialogues are usually subdivided into three broad groups.[12] The early dialogues are seen as a means by which Plato can represent and continue the distinctive philosophical method of Socrates (469–399 BC). The chief feature of this method is a type of systematic dialogue or dialectic, conducted between Socrates and one other person at any one time (the 'interlocutor'). In a typical early Platonic dialogue, Socrates shows the interlocutor that he holds logically inconsistent beliefs, and leads him towards holding different, more consistent beliefs. Socrates does not claim to know the truth about the matters examined or to be able to teach this to the interlocutor. What he claims to do is to show the other person the way in which truth can in principle be found, namely through logical argument based on sound assumptions. The truth which Socrates seeks is especially that about ethics, which means (in Greek thinking) about human virtues and happiness.[13] In the *Symposium*, Socrates' distinctive method is only displayed at one point (in showing Agathon the inconsistency of his beliefs about love); but Alcibiades and others refer to it as his regular practice.[14]

The *Symposium* is usually placed among Plato's middle-period dialogues,[15] together with *Phaedo*, *Republic* and *Phaedrus*. Characteristic of this period is that Socrates' arguments are more extended and more positive in outcome than in the early period. These arguments focus on certain ideas which are usually seen as central to Plato's philosophy, including the theory of Forms.[16] In the *Symposium*, this theory appears at the end of Socrates' speech, in the 'mysteries' of Diotima (210e–212a). Also characteristic of the middle dialogues, especially the *Symposium* and *Phaedo*, is the presentation of Socrates, through narrative and drama, as an exemplar of virtue. In the *Symposium*, this is most obvious in the speech of Alcibiades at the end of the dialogue, though it is implied elsewhere. Plato's late dialogues are usually longer (they include linked sets of dialogues), and are sometimes more technical and philosophically demanding.

Although the three groups of Platonic dialogues differ in this way, it is possible to argue that they are united by the Socratic idea of philosophy as a continuing search for objective truth.[17] In the middle dialogues, although Socrates presents objective truth (conceived as knowledge of the Forms) as the ultimate target of philosophy, he does not himself claim to have achieved this target.[18] In the *Symposium*, Socrates ascribes knowledge of truth to Diotima, a priestess or prophetess; and what she offers to Socrates, in visionary style, is *the path towards knowledge of the truth*, and not an analysis of what this knowledge consists in. A crucial part of Diotima's visionary message is that achieving knowledge of the Forms depends on developing the right kind of character and way of life as well as using the right kind of philosophical method. In the late dialogues, the Socratic spirit is expressed especially in the fresh examination of key ideas of the middle period, including the theory of Forms. Plato uses new spokesmen and methods to deepen the understanding of those ideas or to explore alternatives to them. His overall aim, in the different types of dialogue he writes, seems to be to promote the philosophical search for objective truth by representing this search and by emphasizing the difficulty or incompleteness of this search.[19]

This may be taken as the underlying goal of the various types of discourse (narrative, speech-making, argument) used by Plato in a dialogue such as the *Symposium*. The *Symposium* represents an encounter between specific historical individuals, including well-known Athenian poets and intellectuals, and the politician Alcibiades. It purports to represent a specific, datable event (a symposium two days after Agathon's first win in the tragic competition in the Lenaean festival in 416 BC). Alcibiades' speech contains highly circumstantial details about Socrates' behaviour on campaign – and in bed. But it is almost certainly a mistake to think that Plato's primary aim is to report a certain set of historical facts; or even to give a particular impression about Socrates and his relations with his contemporaries (though that is a more plausible aim). More probably, Plato's overall aim is to construct out of partly historical materials a kind of drama whose organizing principles are philosophical and not factual. To this extent, Plato's dialogues, despite their historical basis, represent a type of fiction, or what the American writer Norman Mailer called 'faction' (making fiction out of fact). But the purpose of the fiction is not invention for its own sake but to promote, through representation, the continuing search for knowledge of objective truth.[20]

This point helps to explain three striking formal features of the *Symposium* which have been much discussed in recent years. The dialogue has a narrative framework that is extraordinarily complex (though skilfully handled), even by Plato's standards. The outer frame is a dialogue in direct speech between Apollodorus and an unnamed friend (172a–173e). This serves as a context in which Apollodorus narrates the report he heard (from Aristodemus) about the speeches on love made at Agathon's symposium. The frame-conversation emphasizes the difficulty in transmitting this report and the efforts made to obtain it by another person (Glaucon) to whom Apollodorus has already given a report. Apollodorus' whole account is in double indirect speech: in Greek, he frequently says, 'he (Aristodemus) said that he (e.g. Socrates) said', though this is too clumsy to convey in English translation. Also two important conversations, between Socrates and Diotima, and between Socrates and Alcibiades, are in direct speech within the narrator's double indirect speech.[21] Although these formal features can be explained in various ways, one line of interpretation is this. These features suggest the 'erotic' attraction of the search for truth, a search which is exemplified in Socrates' conversations and in his way of life. This explains the eagerness with which these different people try to recover the ideas and the spirit of Socrates' speech about love at Agathon's symposium. The use of a chain of reporters emphasizes the difficulty of gaining

Dialogues vital.

are xviii

even partial and indirect access to the truth (or rather, to the *search* for truth). Also implied, in this way and others, is that making progress in this search (as well as completing it) means that you have to change your overall objectives and adopt the philosophical way of life.[22]

The second striking feature is the extent to which the form of the *Symposium* involves Plato as author in impersonating different mentalities and perspectives on love. Of course, such impersonation is to an extent an integral part of the dialogue form; but the rhetorical character of the *Symposium* requires Plato to impersonate verbal style as well as mode of thinking. Also the fact that the content of the speeches is not examined through Socratic dialogue (this only happens in Agathon's case) means that speeches are allowed to stand without comment to a degree unusual in Plato's dialogues. There are, however, certain indirect judgements slyly inserted by the narrator or other characters.[23] In addition, the main speech of the dialogue, that of Socrates speaking as Diotima, responds to the other speeches, either by contradicting or by extending their approach.[24] These aspects of the dialogue also carry implications relevant to Plato's overall aims as a writer. On the one hand, they imply that all human beings have some sort of grasp (belief, though not knowledge) of ethical truth. On the other, it is implied that this grasp is partial and perspectival compared to Diotima's 'prophetic' insight; and that dialectical understanding is needed to bring this grasp closer to real knowledge.[25] In this respect, the *Symposium* is more like other Platonic dialogues (in which the interlocutors' partial understanding is developed through dialectical scrutiny) than it initially seems.

The third feature is that the main speech of the dialogue, that of Socrates–Diotima, is juxtaposed to a character-sketch of Socrates (by Alcibiades). It is usually supposed that the character-sketch of Socrates illustrates the outcome of adopting Diotima's approach to love, as expressed in her 'mysteries', and that it presents this outcome as beneficial. However, Martha Nussbaum believes that Alcibiades' speech brings out the defects of Diotima's approach and shows the

Thinking is vital.

lack of love which results from following her advice (see further xxxviii–xxxix). Even if we do not accept Nussbaum's view as a whole, there are certain hints in the dialogue that we should have reservations about Diotima's confident presentation of knowledge of truth (at least, of how to achieve such knowledge). Also Diotima's prophetic, almost god-like, status marks her level of understanding as virtually beyond the reach of mere human beings.[26] In this respect too, the form of the *Symposium* underlines the general Platonic theme that philosophical enquiry (and the associated way of life and character) consists in a continuing *search* for knowledge of objective truth rather than in its achievement.

The First Three Speeches

Each person at the symposium agrees to make a speech in praise of love, or, more precisely, Love or Eros, as a god. The speech of praise (eulogy or encomium) is a standard ancient rhetorical form. Guidelines for this type of speech are given in a rhetorical treatise of around 300 BC; and the eulogies in the *Symposium* are clearly modelled on this pattern. The eulogy should include: (1) the origin or genealogy of the subject, or noble birth; (2) good qualities other than virtues, such as strength and beauty; (3) virtues such as wisdom, justice, courage and 'practices that win reputation'; (4) habits and way of life; (5) achievements of the subject, by contrast with those of others.[27] The speeches also assume that the proper form of relationship between god and worshipper is that of reciprocity.[28] The praise to Love (Eros) offered by the speakers is a form of worship or benefit that should earn the god's reciprocal benefit to them.

Phaedrus' speech is the shortest and in many ways least adequate, although his wish to have Love eulogized is the starting point for the whole series. His speech focuses on two of the standard themes of the eulogy: genealogy and achievements or benefits of Love. He presents Love as among the oldest, or the oldest, of gods; and also as the god that provides most benefit to human beings. This benefit takes the form of promoting virtues in human beings, especially courage, as expressed in dying for the one you love. Phaedrus' key point is that 'it's only lovers (*erôntes*) who are willing to die for someone else' (179b). His main examples are rather surprising because they consist of what are, in Greek terms, 'loved ones' (*erômenoi*) rather than 'lovers' (*erastai*), namely Alcestis, dying for her husband Admetus, and Achilles, dying to avenge Patroclus. Phaedrus' consistency can be preserved if we take 'lovers' (literally, 'those loving') to include both 'lover' and 'loved one', and acknowledge (as other speeches do) that the loved one becomes virtuous through being loved.[29] But, even so, he develops these ideas in a rather oblique and unargued way. The overall impression is that the speech is characterized by rhetorical effects and 'lateral thinking' rather than strict logic.

Pausanias' speech is more strongly argued, though it is questionable in one salient respect. This speech has the special interest that, more than perhaps any other single ancient source, it presents what most scholars see as a prevalent pattern of male–male sexual relations in Classical Athens, especially the erotic-educational version of this pattern. It also seems to be a means through which Plato, by implication, criticizes this pattern.[30] Pausanias contrasts Greek societies in which there is blanket approval of this type of love (for instance, Elis and Boeotia) and those in which there is blanket disapproval (Ionia). He also highlights a 'double standard' applying to male–male relations in Athens: on the one hand, the lover's pursuit of loved boys is encouraged, while, on the other, fathers try to protect their sons from lovers' attentions. Foucault, as noted earlier, explains this kind of ambivalence by reference to the problematic status of sexual relations between free, citizen males.[31] Pausanias, however, explains it by reference to a distinction between better and worse types of Love, which he calls Heavenly and Common Love. The apparently ambiguous attitude of Athenians towards male–male sexual relations is presented as allowing time to determine whether the love involved is Heavenly or Common and therefore to be encouraged or prevented.

Common Love is purely physical; Heavenly Love is also physical, but it is only aroused by those who are capable of rational and ethical development. Thus, Common Love is directed equally at women (taken to be non-rational) or boys, whereas Heavenly Love is directed only at males who have reached the age (adolescence) at which they become capable of developing rationality and virtue. Pausanias presents the relationship (in a way that partly reflects wider social attitudes) as a form of reciprocity in which the ethical education of the youth is exchanged for the sexual gratification of the man.[32] For this pattern to make full sense, the man as well as the youth should want to carry this education forward. But Plato makes Pausanias emphasize, rather, the lover's concern with sexual gratification (within this type of relationship), by contrast with the young man's concern with his own education. In doing so, Plato as author is probably highlighting the contrast with the type of educational-erotic relationship advocated later by Socrates–Diotima, in which the physical dimension of love is wholly absent and the lover is positively motivated to promote the boyfriend's virtue.[33]

Eryximachus, like Pausanias, distinguishes good and bad kinds of love; but, unlike Pausanias, he broadens the scope of love to include all human and natural processes (186a). This feature of his speech is probably the most significant and suggestive. It anticipates the 'cosmic' conception of love (embracing human and animal desire) of Diotima, though, like Diotima's theory, it raises the question whether love is still the topic of discussion. However, that question is raised more acutely in Eryximachus' case because he shifts rather awkwardly between different ideas and approaches. Pausanias had said that it was right *for the boyfriend* to gratify moderate but not self-indulgent lovers. Eryximachus reuses this distinction from a quite different standpoint, saying that it is right *for the expert* to gratify moderate desires but not self-indulgent ones, a point made in connection with medicine, music (as applied to people) and religious ritual.[34] But this is combined, in turn, with the quite different idea that the function of these and other types of expertise is to combine potentially antagonistic or discordant elements and to create harmony between them.[35] These two ideas can perhaps be reconciled. The common theme is the ideal of the 'well-ordered' (*kosmios*) or harmonious: well-ordered desires should be gratified and order is created by harmonizing contrasting elements.[36] But Eryximachus does little to recognize this difference between his two themes or to work out a proper relation between them.

What is the overall impact of this speech? Throughout the dialogue, Eryximachus is characterized as rather pompous, over-emphatic about his expertise as a doctor and in his role in imposing 'orderliness' on the conduct of the symposium. Those same features reappear in the speech.[37] The latter point is satirically underlined by Aristophanes' comment that the success of Eryximachus' sneeze-treatment for curing hiccups hardly matches his claims about the 'well-ordered' character of the body (189a). The speech gives the impression of someone who is so preoccupied with his own expertise that he imposes it unsuitably on his subject. Also, in his concern to impose 'order' on his topic, he fails to notice that different themes and standpoints are awkwardly combined. Plato may be using Eryximachus to satirize the intellectual pretensions (as he sees it) of medical experts in his day.[38] Within the context of the *Symposium* itself, Plato may be suggesting that you cannot be successful in providing a cosmic view of love if you limit your treatment to the body and physical elements, as Eryximachus does. You need to include the dimensions introduced by Diotima (mental as well as physical love, an overall theory of human and animal desire, the Form of Beauty as an ultimate goal) if you are to place human love convincingly in a cosmic setting.

Love is universal.

The Speeches of Aristophanes and Agathon

Whatever the underlying point is of the choice and order of the first three speeches, that of the next two is clear. They represent comic and tragic perspectives on love, both of which are explicitly criticized or rejected by Socrates.[39] Aristophanes' speech consists of an extravagant and entertaining myth, claiming to explain the power of love (understood as sexual desire for a specific person) in human lives. In his myth, human beings were originally double their present shape and size (they had four arms, two faces and so on); they were also of one of three genders – male, female and hermaphrodite. Because these powerful creatures threatened divine power, they were cut in half by Zeus, and human beings – we are warned – may be cut in half again unless they are orderly and respectful to the gods. This myth explains 'the innate desire of human beings for each other' (191d). Sexual preference for one or other gender (which Aristophanes presents, perhaps surprisingly, as exclusive and lifelong)[40] is explained by the type of combination from which we were split. The myth also explains the intensity of feeling aroused by sexual love: our essential desire, Aristophanes claims, is to reconstruct our original human compound by finding our own 'other half' and by rebuilding that compound, as far as possible, through physical love.

Many modern readers find this the most appealing of all the speeches in the *Symposium*, and more so than that of Socrates. But what is its point? Some scholars stress what seems to be an implication of the myth: that, since we are looking for our other half, love is directed at *individuals*. Nussbaum, for instance, finds here an expression of the idea (markedly absent in Socrates' speech) that love is a response to another person's unique *individuality*, by contrast with her qualities. However, the myth tells us little or nothing about what such individuality consists in. The point stressed is not so much that people respond to their other halves as distinct 'others' but as halves who are 'their own'. The concluding advice is that, given the unlikelihood of recovering our own other half, we should look for 'a loved one who naturally fits your own character' (193c), that is, presumably, one whose qualities are similar to our own.[41]

If the myth is not about love as a response to unique individuality, what is it about? A central image of the myth is of people trying to reconstitute their original unity by sexual intercourse and by physical and social proximity.[42] Another motif is that people do not themselves understand the reason for the intensity of erotic attraction, but 'like an oracle' 'half-grasp' the reason (192d). As Aristophanes implies, in his exchanges with Eryximachus, his myth has serious content, in spite of its comic style (193b, d, cf. 189b). Like Socrates–Diotima, he claims to disclose a motive for erotic attraction and sexual intercourse of which people are only partly aware (192c). In Socrates' case, as we shall see, this is the desire to achieve self-immortalization through procreation. For Aristophanes, it would seem, the explanation is that sexual intercourse is a key part of living a 'shared life' (192d–e). The 'shared life', together with reciprocity, is a central ideal in Greek thinking about interpersonal relations.[43] Aristophanes' myth can be seen as explaining the characteristic symptoms of erotic passion (sexual intercourse and so on) by the desire to achieve this ideal, described as a way of re-creating our 'original natural state' (192e). This ideal necessarily implies that we share our (finite) lives with another *individual*. But the emphasis is, I think, not so much on this individuality but on the fundamental character of the human motivation to lead a 'shared life'.

If Aristophanes' comic speech has a serious message (though not one endorsed by Socrates), Agathon's tragic one is striking for its showiness and superficiality. In fact, it seems more rhetorical than tragic. Socrates comments subsequently on the influence of Gorgias, the famous teacher of rhetoric; and the speech displays several features of Gorgias' rhetoric, including self-conscious artfulness, paradox and verbal display. However, the speech also includes poetic imagery and quotation (195d–e). It concludes (after a verse couplet) with a prose-poem, in which rhetorical devices such as assonance and

I know where Aristophanes begins.

balanced clauses are combined with metrical patterns.[44] This way of characterizing the tragic view of love may reflect a more general tendency in Plato's dialogues to present tragedy as a fundamentally superficial genre, designed to produce an emotional impression without real knowledge of the ethical content of the actions represented.[45] It is surely not accidental that, in the exchanges between Agathon and Socrates, the contrast is stressed between deep and shallow wisdom or between obscure and brilliant (or 'showy') wisdom.[46] We are left with the impression of someone with a rather narcissistic self-regard, who aims at the appearance of wisdom. This impression is connected, as I shall explain, with his account of love as supremely beautiful, and thus like a loved one rather than a lover.

Agathon's speech, like that of Phaedrus, follows closely the 'textbook' rules for a eulogy summarized earlier. He presents first the origin of Love (arguing, against Phaedrus, that he is the youngest of the gods); then his good qualities other than virtue, especially his beauty; then his virtues; and finally his benefits to humanity. Phaedrus' speech seems to be marked by a certain rhetorical looseness of thought. In Agathon's case, this becomes wilful sophistry on each of the topics he covers. For instance, whereas Phaedrus saw Love as promoting virtues in humans, Agathon uses a series of fallacies to ascribe all the main virtues to Love.[47] But the most marked feature of Agathon's speech is the way his characterization of Love recalls himself. From the start of the dialogue, Agathon is depicted as physically beautiful, a suave host with the social graces, and as someone with pretensions to 'wisdom' (especially in his tragic poetry). In his presentation of Love, Agathon stresses these same features, and does so in the self-consciously 'clever' style noted earlier.[48] In the partnership with Pausanias, Agathon clearly plays the role of the 'loved one' rather than the lover.[49] So his attribution of his own characteristics, above all beauty, to Love contributes to the point on which Socrates fastens: that Agathon sees Love as the loved one not the lover.

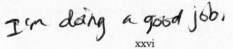
I'm doing a good job.

Socrates and Diotima

The speech of Socrates is the philosophical climax of the dialogue. Despite Socrates' negative comments about the previous speeches (198d–e), his own speech alludes to, modifies or corrects those speeches, and in this way he suggests that they have provided some access to the truth about love. Socrates' contribution breaks down into three main parts: his dialectical contradiction of Agathon, his report of Diotima's theory and the 'final mysteries' of her theory. However, all three parts make up part of a continuous argument, and it is worth outlining the overall form of this argument before examining its stages more fully.

(1) Socrates argues (contradicting Agathon) that love or desire is relational and expresses lack or deficiency; love is not beautiful but is desire *of* beauty (199c–201c). (2) Diotima introduces the category of intermediate or mediating entities. These include Love, seen as a 'spirit' mediating between mortal and immortal, combining need and resource (201e–204c). (3) Diotima analyses love as expressing a more fundamental desire: that for perpetual possession of the good or happiness (204d–206a). (4) The specific way in which love satisfies this fundamental desire is by giving birth in beauty and thus gaining self-immortalization (i.e. *perpetual* possession of the good, 206b–208b). (5) She contrasts physical and mental ways of immortalizing yourself, claiming that the latter are more effective in achieving their goal (208c–209e). (6) In her 'final mysteries', Diotima advocates the ascent of desire from physical to mental types of beauty, culminating in knowledge of the Form of Beauty. Giving birth in that type of beauty is presented as the most effective way of immortalizing yourself and thus achieving the highest possible human happiness (210a–212b). A crucial question raised by this argument is whether Socrates–Diotima is still talking about 'love' in the same sense as most of the other speakers or rather about the underlying structure of human (and animal) desire and motivation. This question is raised

acutely by the 'final mysteries' but emerges also at an earlier stage in the theory (especially stage 3).

(1: 199c–201c) In responding to Agathon, Socrates uses his characteristic method of dialectic. He gets Agathon to agree to certain points which are inconsistent with Agathon's original idea (that love is beautiful), and so leads him to abandon this idea. Here and throughout his speech, Socrates relies on the fact that the Greek word *erôs* means (interpersonal) 'love' as well as 'desire' both in a narrow sense ('sexual desire') and a broad one. He argues that love is essentially relational: that is, love is always *of* something. Love is *of* something that you need and are deficient in; so love is also essentially a state of deficiency or need (this idea is more plausible if you think in terms of 'desire'). On this basis, Socrates concludes that love is not itself beautiful, as Agathon had said. Love is *of* beauty (or the good) and therefore it lacks and needs beauty.

Although this initial stage of the argument may seem relatively straightforward and technical, it is both highly controversial and fundamental for the rest of the argument. It would have been possible, for instance, for Socrates to define 'love' in terms of the relationship *between* lover and loved one, or of responses *common* to the two partners.[50] Socrates' focus on the motivation of the lover (not the loved one) prepares the ground for the analysis of 'love' in terms of an individual's pursuit of happiness (stage 3). It also prepares us for the 'final mysteries', in which attention is directed primarily at the lover, and at the progressive modification of his desires, rather than at the relationship between lover and loved one.

Agathon accepts the force of Socrates' conclusion but, clearly, does not want to continue the argument (201c). So Socrates introduces the figure of Diotima, and continues by reporting an alleged conversation with her. She takes Socrates' place in the dialogue, asking the leading questions, while Socrates takes the place of Agathon. Diotima seems to be a purely fictional figure (at least, she is used for the purposes of Plato's fiction);[51] Plato has several reasons for introducing her. It enables Socrates to continue to develop his argument; the stages of the theory are signalled by interchange between the two figures. Also Plato uses this prophetic figure to provide a visionary theory of love from a god-like, authoritative standpoint. But, while doing so, Plato preserves Socrates' status as a *searcher* for knowledge and one who claims to 'know nothing'.[52] In certain ways, Plato's use of this figure is paradoxical and surprising. By ancient Greek standards, it is surprising to find a woman adopting a position of authoritative wisdom. Also, although her theory of love is centred on the ideas of pregnancy and childbirth, the highest types of pregnancy and childbirth are located within the male–male erotic-educational relationship.[53] However, these features match a theory which seems designed to challenge virtually all conventional thinking about love, including that based on standard gender roles.

(2: 201e–204c) Diotima's first move is to explain that we should not think that, if Love is not beautiful and good, he is therefore ugly and bad. Rather, Love falls into a category that is intermediate between such opposites. On the same basis, Love is neither a god (assumed to be beautiful and good) nor a mortal but an intermediate or intermediary between these two, a 'spirit' (*daimōn*). This point is illustrated by a myth depicting Love as the product of a sexual encounter between Poverty and Resource: Love is always poor (in a state of need) but he is also resourceful in finding ways to satisfy his need. Diotima's description of the spirit Love is strongly evocative of Socrates (for instance, 'tough, with hardened skin, without shoes . . . a lifelong lover of wisdom').[54] This forms a transition to the idea of Love not as wise (as Agathon supposed) but as a *lover* of wisdom or philosopher (*philosophos*). This sequence of ideas is initially rather puzzling; but it prepares us for the ideas suggested later in the dialogue that the pursuit of true wisdom is the highest form of love and that Socrates is the key example of this kind of love.[55] Here, the initial conclusion is that Love should not be identified with the object of love (as Agathon had done) but with the lover. The intermediate status (in need but resourceful and so on) is that of the lover, searching for his goal; and this, Diotima claims, is also the nature of Love (204b–c).

(3: 204d–206a) Diotima next explains the underlying motive of love, as she sees this. The lover's love of beauty is an expression of the general human desire to gain possession of good things and so to be happy. She rejects the idea suggested earlier by Aristophanes that the underlying motive of love is to find one's own other half, arguing that love is directed not at 'one's own' but at what is good. In effect, Diotima redefines the meaning of 'love' (or 'desire', *erôs*), saying that love *is*, essentially, this general desire for happiness (205d). Our tendency to use the term 'love' only in connection with sexual or emotional relationships between people is a selective use of a term which really has a more general meaning. Diotima draws on this more general meaning to clarify the motivation of the impulse we *do* normally call 'love' (206b). She also shows later how the same kind of motivation is at work in other forms of human activity, which we do not normally associate with 'love' (for instance, the pursuit of fame, or poetry and law-giving, 208c–d, 209d–e).

(4: 206b–208b) The summary of stage 3 in the previous paragraph left out one crucial detail. Diotima restates the overall goal of love as being possession of good things *forever* (205a, 206a). Although she offers no separate argument for this addition, it plays a key role in the next stage of her theory. She redefines the purpose of love (meaning, initially at least, what is normally meant by 'love') as 'giving birth in beauty both in body and in mind' (206b). This desire for reproduction is explained, in turn, by the desire to come as close as we can to achieving immortality along with the good, and in that way to gain possession of the good *forever* (206e–207a). The most obvious expression of this is the desire for sexual reproduction, a desire only stimulated by the presence of a beautiful partner. Diotima argues that the desire for self-immortalization underlies the desire to reproduce, in animals as well as humans; this explains, for instance, why animals as well as humans are prepared to suffer and die to preserve their offspring (207a–b). What lies behind this desire, she maintains, is the temporary and transient character of mortal existence. This affects our mental and psychological as well as physical state: only to a limited degree are we 'the same person' throughout our lives. Reproduction provides the means through which mortal creatures can gain the immortality which is not otherwise available to them, and this is the underlying motive of sexual desire.[56]

(5: 208c–209e) The same explanation is offered for a range of human activities, not all of which are normally described as 'love'. These include the desire for immortal fame, which motivates people to die for others. (Diotima here reuses Phaedrus' examples, and supplements his explanation: that people are willing to die for others out of love for them.)[57] A general distinction is drawn between those who are naturally inclined to reproduce themselves in body and those who do so in mind. This distinction recalls Pausanias' distinction between Common and Heavenly Love.[58] One of Diotima's examples of reproduction in mind also recalls the type of love-relationship praised by Pausanias, in which the lover is attracted by a boyfriend who combines physical and mental beauty. There is, however, the significant difference that, here, the lover's motivation is directed only at making the boyfriend better and not also at sexual gratification. The ethical improvement of the boyfriend is described as the means by which the lover can immortalize himself through the mental 'children' produced by their relationship.[59] A more extended form of mental reproduction is the immortalization of wisdom through 'fathering' poems or laws for one's community.[60]

In the latter three stages of her theory (3–5), Diotima sometimes discusses what is normally called 'love' (erotic interpersonal attraction) and sometimes discusses very different types of motive. Her claim is that all these motives express 'love' in the form of the underlying desire specified earlier, the desire to gain immortality along with the good (206e–207a). Another way in which Diotima revises normal categories is in the way she uses sexual and reproductive language. Both genders are described as 'pregnant'; sexual intercourse is described as a kind of 'childbirth'; and the prospect of childbirth produces quasi-sexual reactions (206c–d). In homo-erotic relationships, the lover's development of the boyfriend's virtue is described as the joint rearing of the (mental) children of their erotic partnership (209b–c). Normal gender distinctions are erased as both genders (but especially the male) take on a type of hermaphroditic status. In particular, the homo-erotic-educational relationship (which is, in effect, a purely *male* relationship) is given precedence over male–female sexuality as the highest form of reproduction.[61]

Diotima's Final Mysteries

(6: 210a–212b) In the final stage of her theory, Diotima moves even further from conventional thinking about love, though just how far she moves is open to debate. These 'final mysteries' (the language evokes the final revelation in Greek mystery religions) have long been regarded as the most important and original part of Plato's thinking about love in the *Symposium*.[62] But this is also the most generalized and visionary part of Diotima's speech. Platonic scholars hold very different views about how to interpret the implications of this section.

What is clear is that Diotima is describing a set of stages (an 'ascent') by which we can reach the highest form of love. This ascent consists, broadly speaking, of a movement from the physical to the mental, and from the particular to the universal. There are two principal types of progression: generalization within each stage and ascension between stages. Diotima seems to begin with the kind of erotic-educational relationship described in the previous stage (209b–c), in which the lover responds to a boyfriend who combines physical and mental beauty by offering ethical advice. In the ascent, the two aspects of this response are separated, and there is generalization in each aspect. The lover is led first to respond to physical beauty, and then to recognize what is in common to all physical beauty, and in this way to reduce his passion for just one body. He should then see mental beauty as more valuable than physical, and repeat the same process in that context. The lover should first respond to the beauty of a particular boyfriend by trying to educate him. Next, he should recognize the mental beauty embodied in social practices and laws, and then that in forms of knowledge, thus reducing his attraction to a single individual (210a–d).[63]

The ultimate stage in this ascent is the recognition of beauty in itself. Diotima's description of this type of beauty unmistakably suggests what is generally called Plato's 'theory of Forms'. Though never fully expounded in the dialogues, the core of the theory seems to be this. There are certain 'Ideas' or 'Forms' which constitute the ultimate, objective ground of being, knowledge and meaning. Here the stress falls on the unchanging, uniform and universal character of the Form. To reach an understanding of this Form is to understand *what beauty really is*, as an objective reality, by contrast with our normally partial and localized grasp of beauty.[64] The recognition of beauty 'in itself' enables the lover to place in a proper perspective the more limited types of beauty that form the earlier stages of the ascent. It also enables the lover to go as far as any human being can in achieving the overall aim of desire in general. By recognizing the true nature of beauty and by gaining contact with its 'divine', immortal being, the lover is enabled to generate 'true virtue' and to become 'immortal – if any human being can be immortal' (212a).[65] This outcome is the highest possible way of reaching the underlying goal of love as described earlier: that is, gaining 'immortality along with the good' through reproduction and birth in beauty (206e–207a).

Diotima's account of the ascent of desire raises many interpretative questions. One, much discussed in recent years, is this: what scope, if any, for 'love', in the normal sense (emotional relationships between individuals), is left once we have completed the ascent? The passage has often been read as implying that we should move *from* interpersonal relationships (responding to particular beautiful bodies and minds) *to* love of the Form of Beauty, and to the kind of procreation that this enables. What is being advocated (in this interpretation) is that we discard interpersonal love in favour of the philosophical love of truth and a way of life based on understanding of this truth.[66]

This is perhaps the most obvious way of reading the passage. However, in recent years several scholars, especially A. W. Price, have argued that the whole ascent (and not just its opening stages) can take place within the context of a single erotic-educational relationship.[67] In support of this reading is the fact that Diotima, at several stages of the ascent, says that the lover's developing understanding is expressed in 'discourse' (*logoi*), which may be spoken to the same partner.[68] She also speaks, at a late stage in the ascent, of 'loving boys [or loving a boy] in the correct way'.[69] In this interpretation, what the passage describes is not the replacement of interpersonal love by philosophy, but the deepening of interpersonal love by the lover's growing understanding of the true nature of beauty. In a comparable passage of Plato's *Phaedrus*, we find a clear description of the kind of love-relationship in which knowledge of the truth transforms the life of both lover and boyfriend. However, if this is also the ideal of Diotima's mysteries, it is much more ambiguously expressed than in the *Phaedrus*.[70]

A further feature in the mysteries, which is not fully explained by Price's line of interpretation, is the role of the guide, who leads the lover through the various stages of the ascent. The guide is, presumably, someone (like Diotima herself or Socrates?) who has passed through the ascent to its conclusion. But the guide is not herself involved in any erotic partnership and seems to be motivated only by the wish to share with others the implications of the truth she has discovered.[71] This point will be especially relevant when we consider the connection between the ascent of love described by Diotima and the characterization of Socrates by Alcibiades.

A final question raised by the mysteries is this. Is Plato really saying that *the only way* we can move towards philosophical knowledge of objective truth is through (or within) an interpersonal love-relationship?[72] A possible response to this question is that, here as elsewhere, Diotima's main aim is to give a general account of human desire ('love' in an extended sense). The mysteries suggest that

Any love is acceptable.

philosophically based knowledge of the Forms provides the best possible route to human happiness and thus the highest form of 'love'. The passage, with its visionary and ambiguous language, allows scope for various possible ways of reaching this goal. One way, just considered, is that an educational-erotic partnership is deepened and transformed through the mediation of a philosophically experienced guide. But there may be other possible routes, including the one assumed in the more usual interpretation, in which philosophy gradually replaces interpersonal love. Perhaps the ascent can be made without involvement in interpersonal love at all. But if so (the mysteries seem to suggest), the philosophical pursuit of the truth must draw on the *same kind* of intense, emotional and (in some sense) 'erotic' drive that typically arises within interpersonal relationships. This may be the implied point of the linkage between interpersonal love and the philosophical search for truth that is made in the mysteries.[73]

Alcibiades' speech

After the philosophical profundity of Socrates' speech, Alcibiades' arrival comes as a rude shock. Entering drunk, supported by a courtesan, he disrupts the agreed conventions of their symposium; his speech reintroduces the ways of thinking about love that Diotima's theory had excluded or transformed. Despite this, there is a clear connection between his speech and that of Socrates–Diotima. Although (significantly) he came in too late to hear that speech, his eulogy of Socrates brings out the fact that Socrates' life and character exemplify the understanding of love expressed in Diotima's mysteries. Alcibiades' speech thus helps us to think about the precise significance of those mysteries by giving a personal illustration of the way of life involved.

Alcibiades sometimes presents himself as praising and sometimes as blaming (or getting his own back on) Socrates; but his speech is mainly praise. Indeed, his speech partly matches the guidelines for a eulogy noted earlier (xx). He first offers through images a general characterization of Socrates, which focuses on the contrast between Socrates' grotesque physical appearance and manner and his real, god-like nature and the powerful effect he has on other people. He then illustrates Socrates' virtues: first his moderation or self-control (*sôphrosunê*), shown in his erotic relationship with Alcibiades, and then his courage (*andreia*) and tough-mindedness, shown in his indifference to pain and absence of fear on military campaign. Finally, Alcibiades restates his opening image of Socrates (the outer–inner contrast) applied now to Socrates' way of speaking in his philosophical discussions.[74]

In so far as this speech offers us a picture of the relationship between two historical figures, it is clearly designed to defend Socrates. One of the most damaging criticisms of Socrates (which may have contributed to his trial and execution in 399 BC) was that he had damaged the character of powerful and controversial politicians such as Alcibiades. This speech suggests that, although Socrates had a strong impact on Alcibiades, it was not decisive. In pressing on with his political career, instead of examining his ethical character through Socratic dialectic, Alcibiades presents himself as rejecting the beneficial influence of Socrates (216a–c). Also, Alcibiades' description of Socrates' calmness and courage in battle (at Delium and Potidaea) highlights the good citizenship of a man executed by the Athenian state (220e–221b).[75]

But, as stressed earlier, Plato's dialogues, although they draw on historical material, use this to construct a 'fiction' whose meaning is primarily philosophical. The key contribution that Alcibiades' speech makes to this fiction lies in the oblique light that it throws on Diotima's speech, especially the mysteries.[76] This is so even though it becomes clear that Alcibiades would not have understood the mysteries even if he had heard them, since his own conception of love is so different. The pattern of loving assumed by Alcibiades is the kind of erotic-educational relationship described by Pausanias, in which the lover develops the ethical character of the boyfriend in return for sexual gratification (184c–185b). When Socrates seems to be erotically attracted to Alcibiades, the younger man encourages him because he wants to get the benefit of being educated by Socrates (217a–b, 218c–d). When Socrates fails to respond as expected, Alcibiades is driven to pursue Socrates, as if he were the lover instead of the boyfriend (217c). When Alcibiades finally gets Socrates alone in bed with him, Socrates comments ironically on the erotic-educational relationship that Alcibiades has in view, describing it, with a Homeric allusion, as the exchange of 'gold for bronze' (218e–219a). Alcibiades also makes it plain that, despite his close physical proximity to Socrates throughout the night, the other man showed no sexual arousal (219c–d).[77]

It seems clear that we are meant to place Alcibiades' description of Socrates against the background of Diotima's speech, especially the mysteries. Socrates, it would seem, has gone far enough up the ascent of love to 'despise' the physical allure of Alcibiades (219c).[78] The central comparison in Alcibiades' speech (Socrates compared to a statue with 'god-like' images of the virtues inside) evokes Diotima's idea that contact with the Form of Beauty enables the lover to give birth to 'true virtue' and to become 'loved by the gods'. Also relevant is Alcibiades' comment that Socrates' discussions contain these images too, and that (if 'opened up') they contain all that you need to examine to become a good person.[79] Other features of Alcibiades' speech confirm the evocation of Socrates in Diotima's picture of Love. Alcibiades' Socrates is a person of 'god-like' (219c) power, whose tough way of life (shoeless, often in the open air) reflects his intense search for wisdom.[80]

If Socrates is as sexually indifferent to physical beauty as Alcibiades suggests, why does he give the impression of being attracted by handsome young men? This feature of Socrates' behaviour, stressed by Alcibiades, is confirmed by Socrates' rather flirtatious behaviour before and after Alcibiades' speech.[81] How are we meant to make sense of these two seemingly contradictory aspects of Socrates' behaviour? One possible explanation is this. Socrates plays the game of erotic-educational love that is current in these circles as a way of arousing the interest of these gifted young men. But he does so only to subvert their expectations by *failing* to show a sexual response when given the opportunity to do so. This produces (as it has produced in Alcibiades) a mixture of humiliation, puzzlement, anger and admiration. It is also designed to stimulate the young men to re-examine their understanding of what 'love' is, although Alcibiades does not go as far as doing this. This technique, if this is what it is, is similar to the way in which Socrates' uses dialectical cross-examination to reduce people to confusion and to realize that they need to reconsider what they think they understand.[82]

If we juxtapose Alcibiades' picture of Socrates to the mysteries of Diotima, how far does this help us to decide between different possible interpretations of what those mysteries imply? For Martha Nussbaum, the mysteries suggest that ascending towards the Form of Beauty requires you to detach yourself from interpersonal relationships. She thinks that Alcibiades' speech illustrates, through Socrates' indifference to Alcibiades' beauty and his ironic treatment of the young man, the kind of detachment from interpersonal love that the mysteries recommend. More unusually, she thinks that Plato as author endorses this criticism of Socrates and the way of life he represents. However, we may see the description of Socrates as supporting the interpretation of the mysteries offered by A. W. Price, in which the ascent deepens interpersonal love rather than replacing it. As Alcibiades is uneasily aware, Socrates wants, and is able, to educate him towards virtue (Socrates 'loves' him, in this sense). It is Alcibiades who 'blocks his ears' and prevents Socrates from fulfilling this goal.[83] The kind of shock tactics just suggested (by which Socrates subverts conventional expectations about what 'love' means) might be seen as a way in which Socrates tries to communicate this kind of 'love' to his 'boyfriends'. In another way, Socrates might seem to resemble the guide, rather than the lover, in Diotima's mysteries, in that he wants to help others to understand the true nature of human happiness, whether or not he is 'in love' with them, in the ordinary sense.[84]

After Alcibiades' speech, the symposium is disrupted again by more revellers and drunkenness; but the narrator recalls two significant images to bring the dialogue to a close. One is the picture of Socrates getting Aristophanes and Agathon (both now very drunk) to agree that someone who has the expertise to write tragedies should also have the expertise to write comedies (223d). Coming as it does at the end of the *Symposium*, Plato's most elaborate philosophical drama, this comment seems to highlight Plato's own skill in combining both comic and serious drama in the service of philosophy.[85]

Secondly, Aristodemus tells how Socrates, having seen the two poets to sleep, washed and spent the rest of the day as usual (presumably in dialectic) before going home to bed. This bears out Alcibiades' picture of Socrates' imperviousness to drink and fatigue in his philosophical search for truth. Also Aristodemus' depiction of himself as faithfully following Socrates conveys the erotic power of Socrates, as an exemplar of the philosophical search; and this returns us to the theme (the erotic pull of this search for truth) from which the whole narrative began.[86]

Notes

1. On the reception of Plato's theory in the Italian Renaissance, see Kristeller (1964), M. J. B. Allen (1984); in late antiquity, see n. 62 below; in Victorian England, see Jenkyns (1980), 281–3; Price (1989), 36–7.
2. See Bremmer (1990).
3. See Davidson (1997), 43–9, 91–7; also Murray (1990); Murray and Tecusan (1995).
4. For a brief but important challenge to this widely accepted view, see Davidson (1997), 167–82; Davidson considers evidence for 'passive' homosexual pleasure and questions the contrast between 'active' and 'passive'

homosexual roles in ancient Greece. The 'active–passive' distinction is sometimes, but not always, found in the *Symposium*; see nn. 29, 49–50 below.

5. See n. 49 below.

6. See Foucault (1987), 187–246; also Dover (1978); Halperin (1990) and
(1996); Winkler (1990).

7. Davidson (1997), ch. 3, emphasizes the wide range of types of (slave)
female prostitutes and courtesans (roughly, 'better-class' prostitutes), and
the wide range of social attitudes towards them in Classical Athens.

8. On the Greek family, see Lacey (1968). The romanticization of male–
female courtship and marriage begins to appear in the Hellenistic and Roman
romantic novel; see Konstan (1994) and Goldhill (1995).

9. For a partial contrast, see Xenophon's *Symposium*, which gives more
prominence to sexual relations between free males and female or male
prostitutes – and wives; see Davidson (1997), 96. Xenophon's *Symposium* is
included in the Penguin Classics Xenophon, *Conversations of Socrates*, ed.
R. Waterfield (London, 1990).

10. See e.g. the speech of Phaedrus (178d–179b); also (more humorously)
of Aristophanes (191e–192b) and Agathon (196c–197b).

11. See *Symp.* 184c–185b, 209a–c, 210a–212a; also *Phaedrus* 249e–256e;
Aeschines, *Against Timarchus* 132–40. For the move by Socrates–Diotima
to appropriate the language of female pregnancy and reproduction for this
male–male erotic-educational relationship, see xxxi–xxxii. This move gives
an added twist to the separation of male and female activities that forms a
background for the homo-eroticism of *Symp.*

12. The three periods are dated as 399–387, 387–367 and 365–347 BC (all
dates approximate) in Kraut (1992), xii. Kraut surveys Plato's work (ch. 1),
treats some key issues, and gives a bibliography. Annas (1996) provides an
excellent short introduction to Plato.

13. See further *Plato: Early Socratic Dialogues*, ed. T. J. Saunders, Penguin
Classics (London, 1987); also Vlastos (1971), (1991), (1994), chs 1–2; Benson
(1992); Penner (1992).

14. See *Symp.* 199b–201c; also e.g. 194d–e, 221d–222a.

15. *Symp.* is usually dated in the period 384–379 BC; see Dover (1965),
(1980), 10.

16. See xxxiii.

17. This is a personal view, though one shared by some other recent
discussions; there is no scholarly consensus about the form and function

of the Platonic dialogues. See further Annas (1996) and n. 19 below.

18. See e.g. *Phaedo* 107a−b, *Phaedrus* 246a, c, *Republic* 506c−e.

19. For recent discussions of Plato's dialogue form, see Griswold (1988); Rutherford (1995); Klagge and Smith (1992); Gill and McCabe (1996), including Gill (1996), which develops the view outlined here; Kahn (1996).

20. On ancient thinking about fact and fiction, see Gill and Wiseman (1993), including Gill (1993), esp. 66−9 on Plato. On the type of evidence available for Socrates and his circle and the problems it raises, see Guthrie (1969), ch. 12; Vlastos (1971), chs 2−3, (1991), chs 2−3; Kahn (1996), ch. 3.

21. *Symp.* 201e−212a and 218c−219a.

22. For the last point, see especially *Symp.* 172c−173d, 210a−212b and 215e−216a. On the narrative form, see Halperin (1992); Osborne (1994), 86−93.

23. See notes on 185c, 189a, 198b−c.

24. See notes on 204c, 205d−e, 208d, 209b−c.

25. On the belief−knowledge distinction in Plato, see Annas (1981), ch. 8; Fine (1992). On the role of dialectic in converting belief into knowledge, see e.g. *Republic* 531e−534d. On possible limitations in Diotima's understanding, see xix−xx.

26. See *Symp.* 204b, 206b, 207c, 208c, 209e−210a, 211d−212a and notes.

27. *Rhetorica ad Alexandrum* (included in the works of Aristotle) 35.

28. For this as a standard assumption of Greek religion, see Parker (1998).

29. On the 'lover−loved one' (or 'active−passive') distinction, see xiv. For the idea that the loved one gains virtue through the relationship, see also *Symp.* 184d−e, 209b−c, 210a, c, 218c−e.

30. See xxxi and xxxii−xxxiv for Plato's alternative ideal. Pausanias seems to have been well known for his lifelong affair with Agathon (see n. 49 below), and so his enthusiasm for a lasting homosexual (educational) relationship may be meant to strike us as rather partisan.

31. Foucault (1987), 187−203; another key ancient text for this topic is Aeschines, *Against Timarchus*.

32. See *Symp.* 184b−185b (for contrasting attitudes to this exchange, see 218c−219a); for a different version of this pattern, see *Phaedrus* 252c−253b, 255a−256e. On reciprocity as a norm in Greek interpersonal ethics, see Gill (1998).

33. See especially 184d−185b (and notes); contrast 209b−c, 210b−c.

34. Contrast *Symp.* 184c−185c with 186b−c, 187d−e, 188c.

35. *Symp.* 186d–187c (noting the rather awkward reintroduction of the other theme in 187c–d), 188a–b.

36. For order or harmony imposed between elements, see 186d–e, 187c; for the idea that 'well-ordered' (*kosmios*) desires should be gratified, see 187d, 188c.

37. See especially 186a–e; also the banality of 176c–d, 185d–e, 214a–c. Note also the absurdity of Eryximachus' claim in 188e not to have 'left anything out' of his coverage, as though inclusiveness by itself was a virtue.

38. On the intellectual aspirations of medical experts at this time (which modern scholars rate higher than Plato probably did) in medical writings of this period, see G. E. R. Lloyd, ed., *Hippocratic Writings*, Penguin Classics (London, 1983), Introduction; also Lloyd (1991).

39. See 199c–201c, 205e. The status of tragedy and comedy as forms of expertise reappears at the end of the dialogue (223d); see xxxix.

40. Sexual preference for gender is more often seen as non-exclusive in Greek thought; see xiii–xiv.

41. For the emphasis on looking for 'their own' (other halves), see e.g. 191a, d, 192b; the phrase 'their own' recurs in Diotima's (dismissive) allusion to Aristophanes' theory in 205e. See Nussbaum (1986), 171–6; for the criticism that this type of interpretation expresses a distinctively modern interest in individuality, see Gill (1990), esp. 77–9.

42. See 191d, 192b–e (Hephaestus offering to reunite people physically).

43. See Gill (1998); both ideals are prominent in, e.g., Aristotle's writings on friendship.

44. See notes on *Symp.* 195a–197e.

45. See especially *Republic* 596–603; see further Ferrari (1989), 120–41; Janaway (1995), ch. 6.

46. See 175d–e, 194a–c.

47. See notes on 196b–197b; also xx–xxi.

48. See 174a, 174e, 175b–e, 194a–c; also 195b–196b (the youth, sensitivity, beauty of Love), 196d–e (wisdom as a poet), 197d (grace and charm at social gatherings).

49. For this relationship as well known, see 177d–e, 193b–c; also Plato, *Protagoras* 315d–e; Xenophon, *Symposium* 8.32. For Agathon as a beautiful 'loved one', see 212e, 213c, 222d, 223a (for the contrast between lover and loved one, see xiv). Pausanias' speech, by contrast, can be seen as validating the role of the erotic-educational 'lover' (see esp. 184d–185c).

50. For instance, Aristophanes defines love in terms of a shared or common desire (192b–e) and Pausanias in terms of a reciprocal pattern, the erotic-educational relationship (see 184d–185c, also 218c–219a). Thus, we should not suppose that the (alleged) Greek tendency to analyse at least homo-erotic love in terms of active and passive roles (xiv) means that 'love' has to be defined as the motivation of the lover.

51. Diotima's existence is not known from any other source. The name Diotima suggests 'honoured by Zeus'; Mantinea may be chosen as her location because it suggests *mantis*, 'prophet'. On the 'fictionality' of the dialogue, see xvii–xviii. This (supposedly earlier) conversation refers to speeches made on this occasion (see 205d–e, also 208d, 209b–c, and notes). The theory of Forms put forward by Diotima in 211a–e is generally attributed to Plato, not Socrates; hence, it is historically implausible that *Socrates* could have learnt it from Diotima.

52. On Socrates as searcher, see xvii; even Diotima confines her mysteries to showing the way to gain knowledge of the ultimate truth, rather than expounding it.

53. This is clear in 209a–c, and may be implied in 210a–212a; see further xxxii–xxxv.

54. 203c–d; see xxxvi on Alcibiades' description of Socrates; also Osborne (1994), 93–101.

55. See xxxii–xxxiv, xxxvii on the mysteries of Diotima and on Alcibiades' speech.

56. The *Symposium* does not refer explicitly to a type of immortality discussed extensively in some other Platonic dialogues, e.g. *Phaedo*, namely that of the disembodied soul or mind, though that type of immortality may be alluded to in 212a (see n. 65 below). See further Price (1989), 30–35, 49–54, who also discusses the ideas about personal identity in *Symp.* 207d–208b.

57. 208c–d, cf. 179b–180b, discussed earlier.

58. 208e–209a, cf. 181b–c.

59. 209b–c; contrast 184c–185c (also 218c–219a), in which the ethical improvement of the boyfriend is the central concern of the boyfriend, rather than the lover, whose attention is focused more on sexual gratification (see xxii).

60. 209d–e: it is less clear, in these cases, what is the beauty which stimulates the reproduction; presumably, it is that of the communities involved.

61. See further Dover (1980), 147; also Burnyeat (1977); Halperin (1990), esp. 262–3, 279–81, 285–92; Pender (1992); Sheffield (unpublished).

62. It served as a source of inspiration for neo-Platonic and early Christian thinkers; see e.g. Plotinus, *Enneads* 1.6.8–9, Origen, *De Principiis* 2.11.7, Augustine, *Confessions* 9.10. On Plotinus' response to the theory of intermediate entities (*daimones*), see Osborne (1994), 112–14.

63. On these stages, see e.g. Moravcsik (1971); Price (1989), 38–42. On the sublimation of sexual desire implied in this process and its relationship to Freudian sublimation, see Santas (1988), esp. 169–72; Price (1990), 250–58.

64. *Symp.* 210e–211c. For other passages on the Forms in the Platonic middle-period dialogues (most of which are also generalized and 'prophetic' in style), see e.g. *Phaedo* 65d–e, 74a–77a, *Republic* 505a–517c, *Phaedrus* 247c–e, 254b–c; for critical analysis (in Plato), see *Parmenides* 129a–135b. See further Annas (1981), ch. 9; Irwin (1989), 90–97; White (1992); Kahn (1996), ch. 11.

65. As in some other Platonic dialogues, immortality for human beings (here presented as only a bare possibility) is seen as the product of an extended process by which the mind or soul becomes 'purified' from the body; see also *Phaedo* 64c–68b, 80a–84b, *Phaedrus* 245c–256e, esp. 249a–d, 256a–e.

66. For this view, see e.g. Vlastos (1981), ch. 1; Nussbaum (1986), ch. 6.

67. See e.g. Kosman (1976); Irwin (1977), 167–9, 234–7, (1995), 310–11; Price (1989), 43–54.

68. 210a, c–d; the virtue 'given birth to' in 212a may include such discourse; however, there seems to be at least one change of partner, from one who has beauty of body to one who has beauty of mind (210b–c).

69. *Paiderastein*, 'boy-loving' (211b) can mean loving one boy or more than one.

70. See *Phaedrus* 252b–256e. Some scholars draw a sharp contrast between *Symposium* and *Phaedrus*, e.g. Nussbaum (1986), ch. 7; Santas (1988), 69–72; others see them as expressing a similar ideal, though less explicitly, e.g. Price (1981), (1989), 55–8; Frede (1993), 410–16. See further, on the issues raised by Nussbaum (1986), chs 6–7: Gill (1990); Rowe (1990); Price (1991).

71. On the significance of the guide, see Gill (1996), 387–90; Osborne (1994), 92–3. The motivation of the guide is a disinterested, non-passionate 'love' which is usually seen as distinctively Christian. Osborne (1994), chs 3–4, suggests that the relationship between Christian and Platonic love is closer than is often supposed.

72. Rowe (1998), 192–3, raises this issue regarding the significance of the mysteries.

73. For parallel suggestions, see Frede (1993), 409–10; Sheffield (2001).

74. *Symp.* 215a–216c, outer–inner contrast; 216d–219e, sexual moderation; 219e–221c, courage and indifference to pain; 221c–222a, outer–inner contrast, applied to Socratic discourse; see also Dover (1980), 164–5.

75. Socrates was tried and executed in 399 BC for 'corrupting the young and not worshipping the gods that the city worships'; there are surviving versions of Socrates' defence-speech ('apology') by Plato and Xenophon. Socrates' association with Alcibiades (and Critias, an anti-democratic politician), contributed to his unpopularity (Xenophon, *Memorabilia* 1.2.12–48). On the trial, see Brickhouse and Smith (1989). On Alcibiades, see also note on 215a.

76. Alcibiades' 'revelation' of Socrates' contemptuous treatment of him in bed seems intended to echo, as well as to illustrate, Diotima's revelation of her mysteries (cf. 209e–210a with 216d–217a, 217e–218b).

77. On homo-erotic conventions and Pausanias' speech, see xxi–xxii. Reciprocity or exchange is a standard Greek way of conceiving friendship – see Gill (1998) and Konstan (1998); what Socrates objects to is the exchange of mental for physical benefit.

78. Cf. 210b–c (also 211d) with 219c (also 216d–e).

79. Cf. 212a with 215b, 216d–217a, 221d–222a.

80. Cf. 202d–203d with 219e–220d (also 215c–e, 219c on his god-like or 'daimonic' power and character); see also n. 54 above.

81. *Symp.* 213c–d, 222c–223a, in which Socrates presents himself as a conventional homo-erotic lover; also 216d–e, 222a–b (in Alcibiades' speech). This is a feature of Socrates' behaviour in some other Platonic dialogues, e.g. *Lysis* 204b–c, *Charmides* 154b–155e.

82. See further Gill (1990), 82. This suggestion relates to Plato's *presentation* of Socrates (here and to some extent in other dialogues). It is much more difficult to say how far it reflects the attitudes and behaviour of the historical Socrates. (Socrates is also presented as critical of the sexual dimension in male–male love in Xenophon, *Memorabilia* 1.2.29, 1.3.8–13, *Symposium* 4.26, 8.12, 8.32.) Plato also rejects the sexual dimension of male–male relationships in *Republic* 403b, *Phaedrus* 256, and (emphatically) *Laws* 636a–c, 836c–841e.

83. See 215e–216c (also 217a, 222a); also 212a. See Nussbaum (1986), ch. 6; Price (1989), 43–54 and (1991); also xxxvi.

84. See 212b (illustrated in his treatment of Alcibiades and other young men); on the significance of the guide, see xxxiv.

85. See further Clay (1975); Patterson (1982).

86. See the opening frame-conversation and xviii–xix.

The Symposium

noun

1. a conference or meeting to discuss a particular subject,

APOLLODORUS: In fact, I'm well prepared to answer your question.[1] 172a
As it happens, the other day I was going to the city from my home
in Phalerum, and someone I know spotted me from behind and
called me from a distance. He said (with playful urgency):

'Hey, the man from Phalerum![2] You! Apollodorus, won't you
wait?'

I stopped and waited.

He said, 'Apollodorus, I've just been looking for you to get the
full story of the party at Agathon's, when Socrates, Alcibiades and   b
the rest were there for dinner: what did they say in their speeches
on love? I had a report from someone who got it from Philip's son,
Phoenix;[3] but he said you knew about it too. He wasn't able to give
an exact report. Please give me your account. Socrates is your friend,
and no one has a better right to report his conversations than you.
But before you do,' he added, 'tell me this: were you at this party
yourself or not?'

'It certainly wasn't an exact report you were given,' I replied, 'if   c
you think this party was recent enough for me to be there.'

'Yes, I did think that,' he said.

'How could you think that, Glaucon?[4] Don't you know that it's
many years since Agathon stopped living in Athens, but it's not yet
three years since I started to spend my time with Socrates and made
it my job to find out what he says and does every day?[5] Before then,
I used to run around aimlessly. I thought I was doing something   173a
important, but really I was in the most pathetic state – just like you

3

now! – thinking that philosophy was the last thing I should be doing.'

'Don't make fun of me,' he said; 'just tell me when this party took place.'

'When you and I were still children,' I said, 'and Agathon won the prize with his first tragedy. It was the day after he and his chorus held a sacrificial feast to celebrate their victory.'[6]

'So it really was a long time ago,' he said. 'Who gave you your report; was it Socrates himself?'

b   'Certainly not!' I said. 'It was the same person who told Phoenix, someone called Aristodemus from Cydathenaeum, a little man who always went around barefoot. He was at the party because he was, I think, one of the people most in love with Socrates at that time.[7] But, of course, I checked with Socrates afterwards some of the points he told me, and he confirmed Aristodemus' account.'

'Come on,' he said, 'why don't you repeat this to me now? After all, walking on the road to the city[8] gives us a good chance to talk and listen as we go along.'

So as we walked along this is what we talked about, and that's
c   why, as I said at the start, I'm well prepared. If I need to go through it for you as well, that's what I must do. In fact, whenever I discuss philosophy or listen to others doing so, I enjoy it enormously, quite apart from thinking it's doing me good. But when I hear other kinds of discussion, especially the talk of rich businessmen like you, I get bored and feel sorry for you and your friends, because you think
d   you're doing something important, when you're not. Perhaps you regard me as a failure, and I think you're right. But I don't *think* you're a failure, I *know* you are.

COMPANION: You're always the same, Apollodorus. You're always running down yourself and other people. You seem to believe that simply everyone is in a sad state except Socrates, beginning with yourself. How you ever got the nickname of 'the softy',[9] I don't know. In your conversation, you're always just the same as you are now, savage in your attacks on yourself and everyone – except Socrates.

APOLLODORUS: Well, my dear friend, it's quite obvious, is it, that   e
if I take this view about myself and you, I'm raving mad?

COMPANION: It's not worth quarrelling about this now, Apollodorus. Please, just do what I asked you, and tell me how the speeches
went.

APOLLODORUS: All right, they went something like this – but it
would be better if I try to tell the story from the beginning, just as   174a
Aristodemus did.

He said that he met Socrates, who'd just had a bath and put on
sandals – things he hardly ever did.[10] He asked Socrates where he
was going looking so smart.

Socrates replied, 'To dinner with Agathon. Yesterday I stayed away
from his victory celebrations, avoiding the crowd; but I promised to
join him today. That's why I've smartened myself up, so that I can
look good when I go to the home of a good-looking man.[11] But
what about you?' he asked. 'How would you feel about coming to
dinner without an invitation?'   b

'I'll do whatever you say,' Aristodemus replied.

'Come with me, then,' Socrates said, 'so we can prove the proverb
wrong, and make it say: "Good men go uninvited to *good* men's
banquets".[12] Homer, after all, doesn't just prove the proverb wrong
but comes close to treating it with contempt. His Agamemnon is
an exceptionally good fighter, while Menelaus is a "soft spearman".   c
But when Agamemnon sacrifices and holds a feast, he makes Menelaus, the inferior man, go uninvited to the banquet of a better man.'[13]

Aristodemus replied to this, 'But I'm afraid that I will also match
Homer's description rather than yours, Socrates, and be the inferior
man who goes uninvited to the banquet of a clever one. If you take
me along, think about what excuse you'll give; I won't admit I've
come uninvited, I'll say you've invited me.'   d

' "The two of us going together on our way" ',[14] he said, 'will
work out what to say. Come on, then.'

After this conversation, Aristodemus said, they went off. But
Socrates fell into his own private thoughts and kept dropping behind

as they went along. When Aristodemus stopped too, Socrates told
e   him to go ahead. When Aristodemus reached Agathon's house, he
found the door open, and was caught in a ridiculous situation. One
of the household slaves met him right away and took him to the
room where the others were lying on their couches; and he found
them just about to have dinner. As soon as Agathon saw him, he
said, 'Aristodemus! You've come at just the right time to have dinner
with us. If you've come for any other reason, put it off. I looked
for you yesterday to invite you, but couldn't find you. But what
about Socrates – why haven't you brought him along?'

When he turned round (Aristodemus said), he saw Socrates wasn't
following after all. He explained that Socrates had brought *him* along,
and that he was coming to dinner at Socrates' invitation.

'I'm very glad you are,' Agathon said. 'But where is he?'

175a   'He was behind me just now. I can't think where he must be.'

'Go and look, slave,' Agathon said, 'and bring Socrates here. And
you, Aristodemus, share Eryximachus' couch.'[15]

A slave washed Aristodemus' hands and feet, so he could lie down.
One of the other slaves came and said, 'Socrates is here; he's retreated
into your neighbour's porch and is standing there, and won't come
in, although I've asked him to.'

'That's odd,' Agathon said. 'Go on asking him in and don't leave
him alone.'

b   'No,' Aristodemus said; 'leave him. This is one of his habits.
Sometimes he goes off and stands still wherever he happens to be.[16]
He'll come soon, I'm sure. Don't bother him, leave him alone.'

'Well, if you think so, that's what we must do,' Agathon said.
'Now, slaves, serve dinner to the rest of us. You generally serve
whatever you like, when nobody is supervising you – and I've never
done that. On this occasion, treat me as your guest for dinner as
c   well as the others, and look after us in a way that will win our
compliments.'[17]

So they started having dinner, but Socrates still didn't come
in. Agathon kept on saying they should send for Socrates, but

Aristodemus wouldn't let him. In fact, Socrates came quite soon (he hadn't taken too long doing what he usually did), when they were about half-way through dinner. Then Agathon, who happened to be lying on his own on the bottom couch, said, 'Come and lie down beside me, Socrates, so that, by contact with you, I can share the d piece of wisdom that came to you in the porch. It's clear you found what you were looking for and have it now; otherwise you wouldn't have stopped.'

Socrates sat down and said, 'How splendid it would be, Agathon, if wisdom was the sort of thing that could flow from the fuller to the emptier of us when we touch each other, like water, which flows through a piece of wool from a fuller cup to an emptier one. If wisdom is really like that, I regard it as a great privilege to share e your couch. I expect to be filled up from your rich supply of fine wisdom. My wisdom is surely inferior – or rather, questionable in its significance, like a dream – but yours is brilliant and has great potential for growth. Look at the way it has blazed out so fiercely while you're still young; it was on display the other day, with more than thirty thousand Greeks there to see it.'[18]

'You're treating me with contempt,' Agathon said. 'We'll argue for our rival claims to wisdom a bit later, and Dionysus will be our judge.[19] But turn your attention to dinner first.'

After this, Aristodemus said, Socrates lay down and had dinner with 176a the rest. They then poured libations, sang a hymn, and performed all the other customary rituals, and turned to drinking. Pausanias took the initiative, saying something like this: 'Well, gentlemen, what's the most undemanding way to do our drinking? I can tell you that I'm in a really bad state from yesterday's drinking and need a rest. I think that's true of many of you, as you were there yesterday – so think about how to do our drinking in the most undemanding b way.'[20]

Aristophanes said, 'You're right, Pausanias, in saying we should cut down the demands we make on ourselves in our drinking. I'm one of those who were thoroughly sodden yesterday.'

They're at a party.

After this, Eryximachus, the son of Acumenus, said, 'I agree with you. But there's still one more person I need to hear from, to find out what stamina he has for drinking, and that's Agathon.'

'I've got absolutely no stamina either,' he said.

c 'It's a stroke of luck for us – I mean, for Aristodemus, Phaedrus and the rest – that you who've got the strongest heads for drinking have given up. We're never up to it. Of course, I don't count Socrates: he can drink or not drink, so it'll suit him whatever we do.[21] Well, since nobody here seems keen on drinking a lot, perhaps you won't find it so tiresome if I state the real facts about getting

d drunk. It has become clear from my medical experience that drunkenness is harmful for human beings. So if I had my way I wouldn't want to go too far in drinking and I wouldn't advise anyone else to do so, especially when you've still got a hangover from the night before.'[22]

Phaedrus of Myrrhinus spoke up at this point: 'I usually follow your advice, especially where medicine is concerned. The rest of us here will do so too, if they're sensible.'

e At this, they all agreed not to make the present occasion a real drinking-session, but just to drink as much as was pleasant.

'Well then,' said Eryximachus, 'now that it's agreed that each of us should drink as much as he wants, without any kind of compulsion, my next proposal is that we should send away the flute-girl who's just come in, and let her play for herself, or for the women in their part of the house, if she prefers, and that we should spend the evening in conversation. Also, if you're willing, I'd like to propose a topic for discussion.'[23]

177a They all agreed and told him to make his proposal. Eryximachus said, 'I want to begin by quoting the *Melanippe* of Euripides: "Not mine the story"[24] that I'm going to tell, but that of Phaedrus here. He often makes this complaint: "Isn't it terrible, Eryximachus," he says, "that the poets have composed hymns and paeans to other

b gods, but none of them has ever composed a eulogy of Love, though he is such an ancient and important god. If you look at our best

8

sophists (for instance, the excellent Prodicus), they write eulogies in prose to Heracles and the rest.[25] Perhaps that's not so very surprising; but I once found a book by a clever writer in which salt gets amazing praise for its beneficial properties, and you can find encomia to many other such things. It's terrible that people have given serious attention to subjects like that, but nobody to this day has yet had the courage to sing the praises of Love as he deserves. Such a great god and so neglected!"[26] I think Phaedrus is quite right on this point. I'd like to please him by making a contribution to this project; also this seems a good occasion for those of us here to celebrate the god. If you agree, we won't need anything to occupy us but discussion. I propose that each of us should make the finest speech he can in praise of Love, and then pass the topic on to the one on his right. Phaedrus should start, because he is in the top position, and is also the originator of the topic.'[27]

'Nobody will vote against you, Eryximachus,' Socrates said. 'I certainly couldn't refuse, since the subject of love is the only one I claim to understand. Nor could Agathon and Pausanias; nor could Aristophanes, whose whole occupation is centred on Dionysus and Aphrodite;[28] nor could anyone else I see here. Of course, this arrangement isn't fair on those of us whose positions come last. But if the first comers say all that is required and do it well, that will satisfy us. Good luck to Phaedrus as he starts off and makes his eulogy of Love!'

All the rest agreed with this and told Phaedrus to do as Socrates said. Of course, Aristodemus didn't remember all that each speaker said and I don't remember all he said. But I'll tell you the speeches of the people he remembered best and that I thought most important.

As I say, Aristodemus told me that Phaedrus spoke first, starting along these lines: saying that Love was regarded by humans and gods as a great and awesome god for many reasons, especially his origin.

'The god', he said, 'is held in honour because he is one of the most ancient, as is proved by this fact: Love has no parents and none

Speech is important

are ascribed to him by prose writers or poets. Hesiod says that first Chaos came into existence,

> and then
> Broad-breasted Earth, a secure seat for everything for ever,
> And Love.

Acusilaus agrees with Hesiod, saying that after Chaos two things came into existence, Earth and Love. On his origin, Parmenides says that "the very first god she devised was Love".[29] So Love's great antiquity is widely accepted.

c

'Because of his antiquity, he is the source of our greatest benefits. I would claim that there is no greater benefit for a young man than a good lover and none greater for a lover than a good boyfriend. Neither family bonds nor public status nor wealth nor anything else is as effective as love in implanting something which gives lifelong guidance to those who are to lead good lives. What is this? A sense of shame at acting disgracefully and pride in acting well. Without these no individual or city can achieve anything great or fine.

d

'Take the case of a man in love who is caught acting disgracefully or undergoing something disgraceful because he fails to defend himself out of cowardice. I think it would cause him more pain to be seen in this situation by his boyfriend than by his father, his friends or anyone else. We see the same thing in the case of the boyfriend: he feels most ashamed in front of his lovers when he is caught in some disgraceful situation. If there was any mechanism for producing a city or army consisting of lovers and boyfriends, there could be no better form of social organization than this: they would hold back from anything disgraceful and compete for honour in each other's eyes. If even small numbers of such men fought side by side, they could defeat virtually the whole human race.[30] The last person a lover could bear to be seen by, when leaving his place in the battle-line or abandoning his weapons, is his boyfriend; instead, he'd prefer to die many times. As for abandoning his boyfriend or failing to help him in danger – no one is such a coward that he

e

179a

Shame is essential.
Love is essential

could not be inspired into courage by love and made the equal of someone who's naturally very brave. When Homer speaks about a   b
god "breathing might"[31] into some of his heroes, this is just the effect that love has on lovers.

'Besides, it's only lovers who are willing to die for someone else;[32] and this is true of women as well as men. The Greeks have adequate proof of this fact in Pelias' daughter Alcestis, who was the only one willing to die for her husband, though his father and mother were still living. Acting out of love, she showed so much more affectionate   c
concern than they did that she made them look like strangers to their son, and relatives only in name. The gods, as well as human beings, saw this as a very fine act. Although many people have performed many fine acts, and although the gods have granted to only a handful of these the privilege of releasing their life again from Hades, they released her life, in admiration at her act. This shows how much even the gods value the commitment and courage that   d
come from love.[33]

'But they sent Orpheus, the son of Oeagrus, empty handed from Hades; they showed him only a phantom of the wife he'd come to fetch and didn't give him the woman herself. They thought he was soft (he was only a musician) because he didn't have the courage to die for his love like Alcestis, but found a way of entering Hades while still alive. They punished him for this, and made him die at the hands of women.[34]

'By contrast, they honoured Achilles, the son of Thetis, and sent   e
him off to the islands of the blessed. He learnt from his mother that if he killed Hector he would then die himself, but that if he didn't he would go home and die in his old age. He had the courage to choose to act on behalf of his lover by avenging him: he not only died *for* him but also died *as well as* him, since Patroclus was already   180a
dead. This won special admiration and exceptional honours from the gods, because it showed how much he valued his lover. Aeschylus talks nonsense when he says that Achilles was Patroclus' lover: he was more beautiful than Patroclus (indeed, he was the most beautiful

of all the heroes), and was still beardless, as well as much younger than Patroclus, as Homer tells us. Although the gods certainly give special honour to the courage that comes from love, they show still
b greater amazement and admiration, and respond more generously, when a boyfriend shows affectionate concern towards his lover than when a lover does towards his boyfriend. A lover is more god-like than a boyfriend because he is divinely inspired. That's why they gave higher honour to Achilles than Alcestis, and sent him to the islands of the blessed.[35]

'That's why I say Love is the most ancient of the gods, the most honoured, and the most effective in enabling human beings to acquire courage and happiness, both in life and death.'

c Phaedrus' speech went rather like that, according to Aristodemus. After Phaedrus, there were some others which Aristodemus couldn't remember very well; so he missed them out and went on to report Pausanias' speech. Pausanias said, 'I don't think our project has been specified properly, Phaedrus, in that we've been told simply to praise Love. If Love were a single thing, this would be fine, but in fact it
d isn't; and since it isn't, it's better to define in advance which type we should praise. I'll try and put things right by stating first which Love we should praise, then giving the god the praise he deserves.

'We all know that Aphrodite is inseparable from Love. If there was a single Aphrodite, there would be a single Love; but since there are two kinds of Aphrodite, there must also be two Loves. And surely there *are* two kinds of Aphrodite? One of these is older and is the daughter of Uranus, though she has no mother: we call her Uranian or Heavenly Aphrodite. The younger one is the daughter
e of Zeus and Dione: we call her Pandemic or Common Aphrodite.[36] So it follows that each type of Love should have the same name as the goddess whose partner he is, and be called Heavenly or Common too. Of course, all gods should receive praise, but we must try and distinguish between the functions of these two gods.

'Every activity in itself is neither right nor wrong. Take our
181a present activity: we could be drinking or singing or discussing. None

Human beings 12 are enabled

of these is right in itself; the character of the activity depends on the way it is done. If it is done rightly and properly, it is right; if it is not done properly, it is wrong. So not every type of loving and Love is right and deserves to be praised, but only the type that motivates us to love rightly.

'Common Love is genuinely "common" and undiscriminating in its effects; this is the kind of love that inferior people feel. People like this are attracted to women as much as boys, and to bodies rather than minds.[37] They are attracted to partners with the least possible intelligence, because their sole aim is to get what they want, and they don't care whether they do this rightly or not. So the effect of love on them is that they act without discrimination: it is all the same to them whether they behave well or not. The reason is that their love derives from the goddess who is much younger than the other, and who, because of her origin, is partly female and partly male in character.

'The other love derives from the Heavenly goddess, who has nothing of the female in her but only maleness; so this love is directed at boys. This goddess is also older, and so avoids abusive violence.[38] That's why those inspired with this love are drawn towards the male, feeling affection for what is naturally more vigorous and intelligent. You can also distinguish, within the general class of those attracted to boys, the ones who are motivated purely by the heavenly type of love. These are attracted to boys only when they start to have developed intelligence, and this happens around the time that they begin to grow a beard. I think that those who begin love-affairs at this point show their readiness to spend their whole lives together and to lead a fully shared life.[39] They do not plan to trick the boy, catching him while he is still young and foolish, and then leaving with a laugh, running off to someone else.

'There should even be a law against affairs with young boys, to prevent great effort being spent on something whose outcome is unclear. In the case of young boys, it is unclear whether they will end up good or bad in mind or body. Good men make this rule for

There are different ways to do things

themselves and are glad to do so. The followers of Common Love should be forced to adopt the same kind of rule, just as we forcibly prevent them, as far as we can, from having affairs with free-born women. These are the men who bring censure on love, so that some people go so far as to say that it is wrong to gratify a lover at all. People say this because they have in view the inappropriate and unjust behaviour of this type of men; surely, there is no action which would rightly be criticized if it were done in an orderly way and in line with the normal conventions.

'The conventions governing love-affairs in other cities are easy to grasp since they have been defined in straightforward terms. But here and in Sparta they are complex.[40] In Elis and Boeotia, and wherever people are poor at speaking, the rule has been laid down straightforwardly that it is right to gratify lovers, and no one, young or old, would say that it is wrong. No doubt, this is to save them the trouble of trying to win over young men by persuasion, bearing in mind that they're incompetent speakers. But in much of Ionia and elsewhere in the Persian Empire the rule is that love-affairs are wrong. In Persia, it is because of their tyrannical government that they condemn them, as well as intellectual and athletic activities. No doubt, it doesn't suit their government that their subjects should have big ideas or develop strong friendships and personal bonds, which are promoted by all these activities, especially by love.[41] In Athens the tyrants found this out by their own experience: it was Aristogiton's love and the strength of Harmodius' reciprocal affection that brought their dominance to an end.[42] So where there is a general rule that it is wrong to gratify lovers, this can be attributed to the defects of those who make this rule: the government's lust for rule and the subjects' cowardice. Where the rule is that it is straight-forwardly right, this is because of the mental sluggishness of the rule-makers.

'Here in Athens our conventions are much better than those; but, as I've said, they are not easy to understand. It is said to be better to love openly than secretly, especially if you love boys of social

14

distinction and good character, even if they are not particularly good looking. Also the lover receives an extraordinary amount of encouragement from everyone, which suggests that he isn't doing anything disgraceful; it is regarded as a fine thing to catch the boy you want and disgraceful to fail. When the lover is trying to catch   e the boy, convention allows him to win praise for doing extraordinary things. If he dared to do these things with any other aim and 183a objective, his reward would be massive disapproval.[43]

'Imagine that someone who wanted to get money from a person, or political office or some other position of influence, was prepared to behave as lovers do towards the boys they love. Imagine that he went down on his knees as a suppliant, begging for what he wanted, and swore oaths, and spent all night on someone's doorstep, and was prepared to undergo the kind of slavery that no slave would put up with. He would be held back from behaving like this by friends and enemies alike; his enemies would criticize him for humiliating   b himself to get what he wanted, while his friends would tell him to stop and be ashamed of what he'd done. But when a lover does all these things, he is indulged and allowed by convention to escape criticism, implying that his objective is wholly admirable. Most remarkable of all, it is widely supposed that the only person forgiven by the gods for failing to keep an oath is the lover. A lover's oath, they say, is no oath at all. So, according to our convention, gods as   c well as humans allow lovers every kind of indulgence. From this standpoint, you would think that in this city it is regarded as wholly admirable to be a lover and to respond affectionately to one's lovers.

'On the other hand, when boys attract lovers, their fathers put attendants in charge of them, with specific instructions not to let the boys have conversations with their lovers. The boys' friends and peer group call them names if they see anything like this going on, and older people don't stop the name-calling or tell them off for   d saying these things. When you look at this, you would think, by contrast, that love-affairs were regarded as wholly wrong here.

'The position, I think, is this. The matter is not straightforward;

Behavior is relevant.

and, as I said before, a love-affair in itself is neither right nor wrong but right when it is conducted rightly and wrong when conducted wrongly. It is wrong to gratify a bad man in a bad way, and right to gratify a good man in the right way. A bad man, in this connection,

e is the lover of the common type, who loves the body rather than the mind. He is not constant, because he loves something that is not constant: as soon as the bloom of the body fades, which is what attracted him, "he flies away and is gone",[44] bringing disgrace on all he said and promised. But the man who loves goodness of character is constant throughout his life, since he has become united with something constant.

184a 'The aim of our practice is to test lovers thoroughly and in the right way, to ensure that boys gratify one type but keep away from the other. That is why, at the same time, we encourage lovers to chase boys and encourage boys to run away from lovers. It's a kind of competition to test which type the lover belongs to and which type the boy belongs to. This explains why it's considered wrong to be caught quickly: this is to ensure that time intervenes, which is thought to be a good way of testing most things. It also explains why it is considered wrong to be caught by a lover's money or political power. In such cases, the boy is either frightened into

b submission by ill-treatment or enjoys the benefits of money or political success and fails to look down on this sort of thing. None of these things are thought to be stable or permanent, apart from the fact that no genuine affection can be based on them.

'Only one way remains, according to our rules, in which it is right for a boy to gratify his lover. I said earlier that the lover's

c willingness to undergo every kind of slavery isn't humiliating or reprehensible. Similarly, according to our rules, there's only one remaining type of voluntary slavery that isn't reprehensible: the type which aims to produce virtue. Our view is that if someone is willing to put himself at someone else's service in the belief that the other person will help him improve in wisdom or some other aspect of virtue, this willing slavery isn't wrong or humiliating.

character's
relevant

'These two rules must be combined (the one governing the love of boys and the one governing the love of wisdom and other kinds of virtue), to create the conditions in which it is right for a boy to gratify his lover. These conditions are realized when lover and boyfriend come together, each observing the appropriate rule: that the lover is justified in any service he performs for the boyfriend who gratifies him, and that the boyfriend is justified in any favour he does for someone who is making him wise and good. Also the lover must be able to develop the boyfriend's understanding and virtue in general, and the boyfriend must want to acquire education and wisdom in general.[45] When all these conditions are met, then and then alone it is right for a boyfriend to gratify his lover, but not otherwise.

'In this case, there's nothing wrong with being deceived; but, in every other case, love is wrong, whether or not you are deceived. Suppose that a boy thinks his lover is rich and gratifies him in the hope of making money; if the lover turns out to be poor and the boy doesn't get any money, what he does is still wrong. This kind of boy has shown something about his character: that he would do any service for anyone to make money, and that is not right. On the same basis, suppose a boy thinks that his lover is a good man and gratifies him in the hope of becoming better through the lover's friendship. If the lover turns out to be a bad person, quite lacking in virtue, there's no disgrace in being deceived in this way. This kind of boy has also shown something about his character: that he's keen to do anything for anybody to gain virtue and become better, and there's no motive more admirable than this. So it's absolutely right to gratify a lover in the hope of gaining virtue. This is the heavenly love that belongs to the Heavenly goddess and is a source of great value to the city and to individuals, because it forces the lover to pay attention to his own virtue and the boyfriend to do the same.[46] All other forms of love derive from the other Love, the Common one.

'This is my contribution on Love, Phaedrus,' he said; 'it's as good as I can manage on the spur of the moment.'

17

When Pausanias came to a pause (I have learnt this kind of word-play from the experts),[47] Aristodemus said, it was Aristophanes' turn to speak. But, as it happened, he was having an attack of hiccups, from overeating or some other cause, and couldn't speak. He said

d   to Eryximachus (the doctor was lying on the couch below his),[48] 'You're the right person either to put a stop to my hiccups or to speak instead of me until they're over.' Eryximachus replied, 'I'll do both. I'll take your place and you take mine when your hiccups are over. While I'm speaking, your hiccups might stop if you hold your breath for a long time; if they don't, gargle with some water. If

e   they're really persistent, get something to tickle your nose with, and make yourself sneeze. If you do this once or twice, they'll stop, however persistent they are.'[49]

'Start your speech as soon as you can,' said Aristophanes, 'and I'll do this.'

Eryximachus said, 'This is what I think: Pausanias started his

186a   speech well but did not carry it through to a proper conclusion, so I should try to complete his line of argument. I think he drew a good distinction in saying there are two kinds of Love. But Love is not only expressed in the emotional responses of human beings to beautiful people, but in many other types of response as well: in the bodily responses of every kind of animal, in plants growing in the earth, in virtually everything that exists. I feel sure it's from medicine,

b   my own area of expertise, that I've realized how great and wonderful a god Love is, and how his power extends to all aspects of human and divine life.

'I'll begin with medicine, to give pride of place to this form of expertise. It's inherent in the nature of bodies that they manifest these two kinds of love. It's generally agreed that bodily health and disease are different states and dissimilar from each other. When things are dissimilar, the objects of their desire and love are dissimilar. Therefore, love is different in the case of a healthy and a diseased body. Pausanias just said that it's right to gratify good people but

c   wrong to gratify self-indulgent ones. It's just the same with the body:

speech is proper.[18]
Medicine is important.

in the case of each body, it is right to gratify the good parts and you should do this (and that's what it means to practise medicine); but it's wrong to gratify the bad and diseased parts and you should deprive them of satisfaction if you're going to be an expert doctor.[50]

'Medicine, in essence, is knowledge of the forms of bodily love as regards filling and emptying.[51] The person who is most of all a doctor can distinguish, within these processes, between right and wrong love. The good practitioner can bring about changes, so that the body acquires one type of love instead of the other; he knows how to implant one type of love, when it isn't there but should be, and to remove the other type of love that is there. He should be able to take the most antagonistic elements in the body and create friendship and love between them. The most antagonistic elements are opposites such as cold and hot, bitter and sweet, dry and wet, and so on.[52] The one who discovered how to implant love and concord between these was our ancestor Asclepius (that's what we're told by poets like those here, and I believe them) and that's how he established the art of medicine.[53]

'Medicine, as I say, is wholly governed by this god, and so are athletics and agriculture; and it's clear to anyone who thinks about it for a moment that the same point applies to music. This is perhaps what Heraclitus has in mind, though he doesn't express it very well. He says about unity that "by diverging, it agrees with itself . . . like the harmony of a bow or a lyre".[54] It is quite absurd to say that a harmony diverges from itself or that it exists while its components are still divergent. But perhaps what he had in mind was that musical expertise creates harmony by replacing a previous divergence between high and low notes with agreement. Surely there can be no harmony between high and low while they are still divergent. Harmony is concord, and concord is a kind of agreement; but agreement cannot be created from divergent things while they are still divergent, and harmony cannot be created unless divergent things agree. Similarly, rhythm is created by replacing a previous

d

e

187a

b

19

c divergence between fast and slow tempo with agreement. Just as medicine creates agreement in one area, music creates it in another, by implanting love and concord between the elements involved; music, in its turn, is knowledge of the forms of love in connection with harmony and rhythm.

'In the structure of harmony and rhythm, considered in itself, it's not difficult to recognize the workings of love; and so the twofold character of love does not show itself here. But when it's a question

d of using rhythm and harmony to produce an effect on people, either by making up music (what they call "composition") or by making proper use of the tunes and verses composed (which is called "education"), difficulties arise and a good practitioner is needed. Here the same principle again holds good: you should gratify and promote the love of well-ordered people, or people who are not yet well ordered but may in this way improve.[55] This love is the good and heavenly one, the love of the Heavenly Muse. But the common

e love is that of the Muse Polymnia;[56] when this type of love is applied, it must be with caution, to ensure that the recipient enjoys the pleasure it provides without being made self-indulgent. Similarly, in my area of expertise, a key part of the job lies in the correct handling of the desires met by the art of cookery, to ensure that people enjoy this pleasure without getting ill. So in music, medicine, and in every other sphere, both human and divine, as far as we can, we must pay careful attention to these two kinds of love, because both kinds are there.

188a 'The character of the seasons is also determined by these two kinds of love. When those elements I mentioned before (hot and cold, dry and wet) are influenced by the well-ordered Love, they are in harmony with each other and achieve a temperate mixture. Their arrival brings good harvests and health to humans and other animals and plants, and causes no damage. But when the lawless and violent Love dominates the seasons, they cause great destruction and

b damage. These conditions tend to produce epidemics and other abnormal diseases for beasts and plants. Frost, hail and blight are the result of the mutually aggressive competition and disorder that is the effect of this kind of love. So what we call astronomy is the knowledge of the workings of love, as these affect the movements of the stars and the seasons of the year.

'Also, all types of sacrifice and the whole sphere of divination (these are the ways in which gods and humans communicate with each other) are wholly directed at maintaining one kind of love and curing the other. Every kind of impiety towards one's parents (living or dead) or the gods tends to occur when people fail to gratify, respect or give pride of place in every action to the well-ordered Love, but do so to the other one. Prophecy has been given the job of keeping an eye on those whose love is the wrong kind and curing this. It also has the job of producing friendship between gods and humans by understanding how the operations of love in human life affect right behaviour and piety.

'So Love as a whole has great and mighty – or rather total – power, when you put all this together. But it is the Love whose nature is expressed in good actions, marked by self-control and justice, at the human and divine level that has the greatest power and is the source of all our happiness. It enables us to associate, and be friends, with each other and with the gods, our superiors.

'It may be that my eulogy of Love has missed out a good deal, but if so this was not intentional. If I have left anything out, it's up to you, Aristophanes, to fill in the gaps. Or, if you have in mind a different kind of eulogy of the god, do carry on, now that your hiccups have stopped.'

Now that it was Aristophanes' turn (Aristodemus reported), he 189a said: 'Yes, they've stopped all right, but not until I applied the sneeze-treatment to them. It makes me wonder whether it is the "well-ordered" part of my body that wants the kind of noises and tickles that make up a sneeze. At any rate, the hiccups stopped right away when I applied the sneeze.'[57]

'My dear Aristophanes,' Eryximachus said, 'be careful what you're doing. By joking before you start to speak, you're making me watch b

out for jokes in your speech too, when otherwise you could give
your speech without interference.'

'You're right, Eryximachus,' Aristophanes said, 'and I withdraw
what I said. But, if you're watching out in my speech, don't think
I'm afraid of saying something funny – that would be pure profit
and typical of my Muse – but of saying something ludicrous.'

Eryximachus said, 'You think you can take a shot at me and run
away! Well, take care; you'll have to answer for what you say. But
c   even so, if I decide to, I'll let you off.'

'Actually, Eryximachus,' Aristophanes said, 'I do intend to take a
different approach from the one taken by you and Pausanias in your
speeches.[58] I think people have wholly failed to recognize the power
of Love; if they'd grasped this, they'd have built the greatest temples
and altars for him, and made the greatest sacrifices. In fact, none of
this is done for him, though he deserves it most of all.[59] He loves
d   human beings more than any other god; he is their helper and
the doctor of those sicknesses whose cure constitutes the greatest
happiness for the human race. I shall try to explain his power to
you, and you will teach this to others.

'First of all, you must learn about human nature, and what has
happened to it. Long ago, our nature was not the same as it is now
but quite different. For one thing, there were three human genders,
not just the present two, male and female. There was also a third
e   one, a combination of these two; now its name survives, although
the gender has vanished. Then "androgynous" was a distinct gender
as well as a name, combining male and female; now nothing is left
but the name, which is used as an insult.[60]

'For another thing, the shape of each human being was a rounded
whole, with back and sides forming a circle. Each one had four
hands and the same number of legs, and two identical faces on a
190a   circular neck. They had one head for both the faces, which were
turned in opposite directions, four ears, two sets of genitals, and
everything else was as you would imagine from what I've said so
far. They moved around upright as we do now, in either direction,

as they wanted. When they set off to run fast, they supported themselves on all their eight limbs, and moved quickly round and round, like tumblers who do cartwheels by keeping their legs straight as they go round and round.

'The reason why there were these three genders, and why they were as described, is that the parent of the male gender was originally the sun, that of the female gender the earth, that of the combined gender the moon, because the moon is a combination of sun and earth.[61] They were round, and so was the way they moved, because they took after their parents. They were terrible in their strength and vigour; they had great ambitions and made an attack on the gods. The story told by Homer about Ephialtes and Otus, how they tried to climb up to heaven to attack the gods,[62] really refers to them. Zeus and the other gods discussed what to do to them and couldn't decide. The gods didn't see how they could kill them, wiping out the human race with thunderbolts as they'd done with the giants; if they did that, the honours and sacrifices the gods received from them would disappear. But they couldn't let them go on behaving outrageously. After much hard thought, Zeus had an idea: "I think I have a plan by which human beings could still exist but be too weak to carry on their wild behaviour. I shall now cut each of them into two; they will be weaker and also more useful to us because there will be more of them. They will walk around upright on two legs. If we think they're still acting outrageously, and they won't settle down, I'll cut them in half again so that they move around hopping on one leg."

'After saying this, Zeus cut humans into two, as people cut sorb-apples in half before they preserve them or as they cut hard-boiled eggs with hairs. As he cut each one, he told Apollo to turn the face and the half-neck attached to it towards the gash, so that humans would see their own wound and be more orderly; Zeus also told him to heal the other wounds. Apollo turned round the face; he pulled the skin from all around the body towards what's now called the stomach (like a purse being pulled tight with a

The gods have 23
contest in our lives.

draw-string), and finished it off by making one opening in the middle of the stomach, which we call the navel. He also smoothed off the other numerous wrinkles, and shaped the chest with the kind of tool used by shoemakers when they smooth the wrinkles of leather on the last. But he left a few on the stomach round the navel, to remind them of what had happened to them long ago.

'Since their original nature had been cut in two, each one longed for its own other half and stayed with it. They threw their arms round each other, weaving themselves together, wanting to form a single living thing. So they died from hunger and from general inactivity, because they didn't want to do anything apart from each other. Whenever one of the halves died and one was left, the one that was left looked for another and wove itself together with that. Sometimes the one it met was half of a whole woman (the half we now call a "woman"), sometimes half a whole man. In any case, they kept on dying in this way.

'Zeus took pity on them and came up with another plan: he moved their genitals round to the front; until then, they had genitals on the back of their bodies, and sexual reproduction occurred not with each other but on the earth, as in the case of cicadas.[63] So Zeus moved the genitals round to the front and in this way made them reproduce in each other, by means of the male acting inside the female. The aim of this was that, if a man met with a woman and entwined himself with her, they would reproduce and the human race would be continued. Also, if two males came together, they would at least have the satisfaction of sexual intercourse, and then relax, turn to their work, and think about the other things in their life.

'That's how, long ago, the innate desire of human beings for each other started. It draws the two halves of our original nature back together and tries to make one out of two and to heal the wound in human nature. Each of us is a matching half of a human being, because we've been cut in half like flatfish,[64] making two out of one, and each of us is looking for his own matching half. Those men who are cut from the combined gender (the androgynous, as it was called then) are attracted to women, and many adulterers are from this group. Similarly, the women who are attracted to men e and become adulteresses come from this group. Those women who are cut from the female gender are not at all interested in men, but are drawn much more towards women; female homosexuals come from this group.[65]

'Those who are cut from the male gender go for males. While they are boys, because they are slices of the male gender, they are attracted to men and enjoy sleeping with men and being embraced by them. These are the best of their generation, both as boys and 192a young men, because they are naturally the bravest. Some people say that they are shameless, but that isn't true. It's not out of shamelessness that they do this but because they are bold, brave and masculine, and welcome the same qualities in others. Here is clear evidence of this: men like this are the only ones who, when grown up, end up as politicians.[66] When they become men, they're sexually attracted by boys; they have no natural interest in getting married and having b children, although they are forced to do this by convention. They are quite satisfied by spending their lives together and not getting married. In short, such people become lovers of boys and boys who love their male lovers, always welcoming their shared natural character.

'When a lover of boys, or any other type of person, meets that very person who is his other half, he is overwhelmed, to an amazing extent, with affection, concern and love. The two don't want to c spend any time apart from each other. These are people who live out whole lifetimes together, but still couldn't say what it is they want from each other. I mean, no one can think that it's just sexual intercourse they want, and that this is the reason why they find such joy in each other's company and attach such importance to this. It's clear that each of them has some wish in his mind that he can't d articulate; instead, like an oracle, he half-grasps what he wants and obscurely hints at it. Imagine that Hephaestus with his tools stood over them while they were lying together and asked: "What is it, humans, that you want from each other?" If they didn't know, imagine that he asked next: "Is this what you desire, to be together so completely that you're never apart from each other night and day? If this is what you desire, I'm prepared to fuse and weld you

e together, so that the two of you become one. Then the two of you would live a shared life, as long as you live, since you are one person; and when you died, you would have a shared death in Hades, as one person instead of two. But see if this is what you long for, and if achieving this state satisfies you."[67] We know that no one who heard this offer would turn it down and it would become apparent that no one wanted anything else. Everyone would think that what he was hearing now was just what he'd longed for all this time: to come together and be fused with the one he loved and become one instead of two. The reason is that this is our original natural state and we used to be whole creatures: "love" is the name for the desire

193a and pursuit of wholeness.[68]

'Before this, as I say, we were unified; but now, because of our crimes, we have been split up by Zeus just as the Arcadians have been by the Spartans.[69] There's a danger that, if we aren't well ordered in our behaviour towards the gods, we'll be split up further, and go around like figures in bas-relief on gravestones, sawn in half down the nose, like half-dice.[70] So everyone should encourage others to show all due reverence towards the gods, so that we can avoid

b one outcome and achieve the other, with Love as our leader and general. No one should work against Love, and to get on the wrong side of the gods is to work against Love. If we are friends of the god and have him on our side, we shall do what few people now do – find and become close to the loved ones that are really our own.

'I don't want Eryximachus to think that my speech is just a comedy, directed at Pausanias and Agathon.[71] It may well be that

c they are among this type and are both halves of the male nature. But what I'm saying applies to all men and all women too: our human race can only achieve happiness if love reaches its conclusion, and each of us finds his loved one and restores his original nature. If this is the ideal, under present circumstances what comes closest to it must be the best: that is to find a loved one who naturally fits your own character. If we want to praise the god who is responsible for this, we would rightly praise Love. In present circumstances, he d does the best for us that can be done, leading us towards what is naturally close to us. He also holds out to us the greatest hopes for the future: that if we show reverence towards the gods, he will restore us to our original nature, healing us and so giving us perfect happiness.

'Well, Eryximachus, this is my speech about love, a rather different one from yours. As I asked you, don't treat my speech as a comedy. Let's go on and hear what each of the remaining speakers has to say – or rather the two of them, as only Agathon and Socrates e are left.'

'I'll do as you say,' Eryximachus said, 'and in any case I much enjoyed your speech. If I didn't know that Socrates and Agathon were experts on the ways of love, I'd be very worried that they might run out of things to say, since we've already had such a wide variety of speeches. But, as things are, I'm quite confident.'

Socrates said, 'That's because you've taken part successfully in our 194a competition. If you were in my position, or rather where I'll be when Agathon too has given a good speech, you'd be very frightened and in just as much of a quandary as I am.'

'You're trying to put a spell on me, Socrates,' Agathon said, 'by making me nervous at the thought that the audience has high expectations of my giving a good speech.'

'But I would have a short memory if I did that, Agathon,' said Socrates. 'I saw the courage and self-confidence you showed when b you went out on to the platform with the actors, facing such a huge audience without any embarrassment, before presenting your own work. So I shouldn't expect you to become nervous in front of our small group.'[72]

'But Socrates,' Agathon said, 'I hope you don't think I'm so

27

Love is universal.
The future is relevant.

obsessed with the theatre that I don't realize that, for anyone with any sense, a small number of intelligent people are more alarming than a crowd of unintelligent ones.'

c 'It would be quite wrong of me, Agathon,' Socrates said, 'to think you could be unsophisticated in any way. I'm well aware that if you found some people you thought were wise, you would pay more attention to them than to the crowd. But I'm afraid we don't fall into that category; after all, we were there and were part of that crowd. But if you found some other wise people, you might feel ashamed if you thought you were doing something wrong in front of them – is that what you mean?'

'That's right,' Agathon replied.

'But wouldn't you feel ashamed if you thought you were doing something wrong in front of the crowd?'

d At this point Phaedrus interrupted and said, 'My dear Agathon, if you answer Socrates' questions, he won't care whether we get anywhere with our present project, as long as he's got a partner for discussion, especially someone attractive. I enjoy hearing Socrates engaging in discussion, but I must look after the eulogy of Love and extract from each one of you a speech as your contribution. So when the two of you have made your offering to the god, then you can have your discussion.'

e 'You're right, Phaedrus,' Agathon said; 'there's no reason for me not to make my speech. Socrates will have plenty of opportunities for discussion another time.

'I want first of all to say how I should speak, then give my speech. I think that all the previous speakers, instead of praising the god, have congratulated human beings on the good things that come to them from the god. Nobody has spoken about the nature of the god

195a himself who has given us these things. There is only one right way of making a eulogy, whatever the topic, and that is to define the nature of the subject of the speech and the nature of that for which he is responsible. So, in the case of Love, the right thing is to praise his nature first, and then his gifts.[73]

Speceh is praised. [28]

'I claim that, though all the gods are happy, Love – if it is proper to say this and does not cause offence – is the happiest, because he is the most beautiful and best. He is the most beautiful for this reason: first of all, Phaedrus, he is the youngest of gods.[74] He himself provides good evidence for this point by fleeing headlong from old age, fast   b
though that is (it comes to us sooner than it should). Love naturally hates old age and keeps his distance from it. He always associates with the young and is one of them; the ancient saying is right, that like always stays close to like. Although I agree with many other things that Phaedrus said, I don't agree that Love is older than Cronus and Iapetus.[75] I claim that he is the youngest of the gods and stays   c
young forever. The things the gods did to each other in ancient times, which Hesiod and Parmenides report, happened (if their reports are true) because of Necessity and not Love. The gods would not have castrated or imprisoned each other or done those many other acts of violence if Love had been among them;[76] there would have been friendship and peace between them, as there is now and has been since Love began to rule among the gods.

'He is young, and sensitive as well as young; but it would take a poet of Homer's quality to bring out how sensitive the god is. Homer   d
describes Delusion as a goddess, and also sensitive; at least her feet are sensitive, as he says:

> But her feet are sensitive; to the ground
> She never draws close, but walks on the heads of men.[77]

I think Homer gives clear evidence of her sensitivity, in saying that she does not walk on what is hard, but what is soft. We can use the same evidence for Love's sensitivity. He does not walk on the   e
ground, nor on skulls (which are not at all soft), but walks and lives in the softest of all things. He makes his home in the characters and minds of gods and humans; and not in all minds, one after another, but whenever he finds one with a tough character he moves on, and whenever he finds one with a soft character he settles down. Since he is in continual contact with the softest members of the

softest type of thing, not just with his feet but with all of him, he must be extremely sensitive.

196a   'So he is very young and sensitive, and is fluid in shape as well. Otherwise, if he was tough, he couldn't envelop someone's mind completely or pass unnoticed at first entry into it and then out of it. Good evidence that he has a well-formed and fluid shape comes from his gracefulness, which is universally accepted as a special feature of Love (gracelessness and Love are always enemies to each other). His beauty of complexion is shown by the fact that he spends his time among flowers.[78] Love does not settle on a body or mind or

b   anything that has no bloom or has lost its bloom; but when he finds somewhere full of bloom and fragrance, there he settles and stays.

'Enough has been said (though still more remains) about the god's beauty; the next topic I must speak about is Love's virtue. The most important point is that Love does no injustice and has none done to him, when dealing with either gods or humans. When Love has anything done to him, it isn't by force (since Love is never forced).

c   When Love does anything, he doesn't use force, since everyone consents to all Love's orders; and whatever is agreed by mutual consent, that is what "laws, the sovereign of the city" define as just.[79]

'As well as justice, Love has the biggest share of moderation. It is generally agreed that moderation is mastery of pleasures and desires, and that no pleasure is stronger than Love. If the pleasures are weaker, they must be mastered by Love and he must be their master; and if Love masters pleasures and desires, he must be exceptionally moderate.[80]

d   'As for courage, "not even Ares can stand up to" Love. It isn't Ares who captured Love but Love who captured Ares (Love of Aphrodite, as the story goes), and the capturer is master of the captured. Whoever masters the one who is bravest of the others must be the bravest of all.[81]

'I've spoken about the god's justice, moderation and courage; it remains to speak about his wisdom. As far as possible, I must try to

Love has many   30
applications.

treat this fully. First of all – to give honour to my expertise in the way that Eryximachus gave honour to his – the god is so skilled a poet that he makes others into poets. Everyone turns into a poet, "even though a stranger to the Muses before", when he is touched by Love.[82] We may take this as evidence that Love is a good composer in, broadly, every type of artistic production, because you can't give someone else what you don't have or teach someone what you don't know yourself. Certainly, as regards the production of living things, who will deny that it is by Love's skill that all living things come into being and are produced? As for expertise in art or craft, don't we know that whoever is taught by this god ends up being famous and conspicuous, while whoever is untouched by the god is obscure? It was by following where his desire and love led him that Apollo discovered the arts of archery, medicine and prophecy, and this makes Apollo a pupil of Love. In the same way, it makes the Muses pupils of his in music, Hephaestus in metalwork, Athena in weaving and Zeus in steering gods and humans.[83] So the activities of the gods only became organized when Love was born among them – love of beauty, of course, as love cannot be directed at ugliness. Before then, as I said at the start, the gods did many terrible things, we are told, under the rule of Necessity. But once this god was born, all good things came to gods and humans through the love of beauty.[84]

'So it seems to me, Phaedrus, that Love is himself supreme in beauty and excellence and is responsible for similar qualities in others. I feel moved to express this in verse and say that he is the one who makes

> Peace among humankind and windless calm at sea,
> Rest for the winds, and sleep for those distressed.[85]

Love drains us of estrangement and fills us with familiarity, causing us to come together in all shared gatherings like this, and acting as our leader in festival, chorus and sacrifice. He includes mildness and excludes wildness. He is generous of goodwill and ungenerous of ill-will. He is gracious and kindly; gazed on by the wise, admired

Love is symphonic.
The Greek men are very wise.

by the gods; craved by those denied him, treasured by those enjoying him; father of luxury, elegance, delicacy, grace, desire, longing; careful for good people, careless of bad people; in trouble, in terror,

e in longing, in discourse, he is the best helmsman, marine, comrade, rescuer. For the whole company of gods and humans, most beautiful and best of leaders; every man should follow him singing beautiful hymns of praise, sharing the song he sings to charm the mind of every god and human.[86]

'There's my speech, Phaedrus,' he said, 'my dedication to the god; it combines entertainment with a degree of seriousness, as far as I can manage.'

198a After Agathon had finished his speech, Aristodemus said, there were shouts of admiration from everyone present, because the young man had spoken in a way that reflected well on himself and on the god. Socrates looked at Eryximachus and said, 'Well, son of Acumenus, do you still think my earlier anxiety was groundless? Wasn't I speaking prophetically when I said just now that Agathon would give an amazing speech and that I would be lost for words?'

'On one point', Eryximachus said, 'you were prophetic, in saying that Agathon would give a good speech; but I don't think you'll be lost for words.'

b 'My good friend,' said Socrates, 'how can I fail to be lost for words, or anyone else, who has to follow such a beautiful and varied speech? The rest was not quite so amazing; but who could fail to be struck by the beauty of language and phrasing at the end? I saw that I couldn't even get close to this degree of beauty in my speech, and was so ashamed I nearly ran away (and would have done if I'd

c had anywhere to go). The speech reminded me of Gorgias, and so I had just the same experience that Homer describes. I was afraid that Agathon would end his speech by directing the Gorgon-like head of the formidable orator Gorgias at my speech and turn me into speechless stone.[87] Then I realized I'd made a fool of myself in

d agreeing to take my turn with you in eulogizing Love and in claiming expertise in the ways of love; in fact I knew nothing about what was involved in eulogizing something. I was so naïve that I thought you should tell the truth about the subject of the eulogy; I thought this should be the basis from which to select the finest features and present them in a way that showed the subject at its best. I took pride in thinking that I would give a good speech because I knew the truth about how to give a eulogy of a subject.

'But in fact, it seems, that isn't the right way of praising something. Instead, you should claim that your subject has the greatest and finest   e possible qualities, whether it really does or not; and if what you say isn't true, it doesn't matter very much. What was proposed, it seems, was that each of us should give the appearance of praising Love, not that we should actually do so. That must be why the rest of you find anything that can be said and ascribe it to Love, saying that he is like this and responsible for that, to make him look as fine and   199a good as possible. You're obviously doing this for the ignorant (not, of course, for those who understand the subject); and your eulogies have certainly been beautiful and impressive.

'But I didn't know the right way of giving a eulogy, and it was out of ignorance that I agreed to give one in my turn. But "it was the tongue" that promised, "not the heart";[88] so let's forget about it. I'm not giving another eulogy of that kind – I couldn't do it. However, I am prepared to tell the truth, if you'd like that, though in my own way, not competing with your speeches, which would   b make me look ridiculous. So let me know, Phaedrus, whether there's any need for a speech like that, one which tells the truth about Love, but which uses whatever words and phrases happen to occur to me as I go along.'

Phaedrus and the others told him to give his speech in whatever style he thought best.

'Phaedrus,' Socrates said, 'would you also allow me to ask Agathon a few little questions, so that I can make my speech on the basis of agreement with him?'

'I give my consent,' Phaedrus said; 'ask away.'   c

After that, Aristodemus said, Socrates made this start to his speech.

'My dear Agathon, I thought you made a good start to your speech, when you said that we should bring out Love's character before turning to the effects he produces. I think that's an admirable way to start. Well then, now that you've given a fine and magnificent exposition of the nature of Love in other respects, tell me this too.[89]

d Is it Love's nature to be love *of* something or nothing? I'm not asking whether Love is the child *of* a particular mother or father; it would be absurd of me to ask whether Love is love *of* a mother or father in this sense. But suppose I'd asked the question, whether a father is father *of* someone or not. If you'd wanted to give the right answer, you'd surely have said that a father is father *of* a son or daughter, wouldn't you?'

'Certainly,' said Agathon.

'The same goes for a mother?'

He agreed to this too.

e 'Well then,' said Socrates, 'answer a little further, and you'll have a better idea of what I've got in mind. Suppose I asked this: is a brother, in so far as he is a brother, brother *of* someone or not?'

He said that he was.

'That is, a brother *of* a brother or sister?'

He agreed.

'Now try to tell me about love', he said. 'Is Love love *of* nothing or something?'

'Of something, undoubtedly!'

200a 'For the moment,' said Socrates, 'keep to yourself and bear in mind what love is *of*. But tell me this much: does Love desire what it is love of or not?'

'Yes,' he said.

'When he desires and loves, does he have in his possession what he desires and loves or not?'

'He doesn't – at least probably not,' he said.

'Think about it,' Socrates said. 'Surely it's not just probable but necessary that desire is directed at something you need and that if

Love has a
character

34

you don't need something you don't desire it?[90] I feel amazingly   b
certain that it is necessary; what do you think?'

'I think so too,' said Agathon.

'That's right. Now would anyone who was tall want to be tall or
anyone who was strong want to be strong?'

'That's impossible, according to what we've agreed already.'

'Yes, because no one is in need of qualities he already has.'

'That's true.'

'Suppose that someone who was strong wanted to be strong,' said
Socrates, 'and someone who was fast wanted to be fast, and someone
who was healthy wanted to be healthy. You might think that in
these and all such cases people who are like that and who have those   c
qualities also desire what they already have. I make this point to stop
us getting the wrong idea. If you think about it, Agathon, these
people must *necessarily* have each of the qualities they have at any
one time, whether they want to or not; and so this can't be what
they desire. So if someone says, "I'm healthy and want to be healthy",
or "I'm rich and want to be rich", or "I desire the things that I've
got", we should say to him, "My friend, you already have wealth   d
or health or strength. What you want is to have them in the future,
since at the present you have them whether you want them or not.
When you say that you desire what you've already got, ask yourself
whether you mean that you want what you've got now to go on
being there in the future." He'd have to agree to that, wouldn't
he?'

Agathon said that he would.

Socrates said, 'What someone is doing in these cases is loving
something that isn't available to him and which he doesn't have,
namely the continued presence in the future of the things he has
now.'

'Certainly,' he said.   e

'So this and every other case of desire is desire for what isn't
available and actually there. Desire and love are directed at what
you don't have, what isn't there, and what you need.'

35

Love acts
on its own accord.

'Certainly,' he said.

'Come on then,' said Socrates; 'let's sum up what we've agreed. First, that Love is *of* something; second, that it is of something that he currently needs.'[91]

201a   'Yes,' he said.

'Now, bearing this in mind, recall what you said in your speech about what Love is *of*. If you like, I'll remind you. I think you said something like this, that the affairs of the gods were organized through love of beautiful things, since it's impossible to love ugly things. Isn't this more or less what you said?'[92]

'Yes, I did,' Agathon said.

'What you say is plausible, my friend,' Socrates said. 'If this is right, then mustn't Love be love of beauty and not of ugliness?'

He agreed.

b   'Didn't we agree that he loves what he needs and doesn't have?'

'Yes,' he said.

'It follows that Love needs beauty and doesn't have it?'[93]

'That must be the case,' he said.

'Well, would you say that something that needs beauty and is wholly without beauty is beautiful?'

'No.'

'If this is so, do you still suppose that Love is beautiful?'

Agathon said, 'It looks, Socrates, as though I didn't know what I was talking about then.'

c   'Ah well, it was still a beautiful speech, Agathon,' he said. 'But answer just one more small question: do you think that things that are good are also beautiful?'

'I think so.'

'Then if Love is in need of beautiful things, and good things are beautiful, he would be in need of good things?'[94]

'I can't argue against you, Socrates,' he said. 'Let's accept that things are as you say.'

'It's the truth you can't argue against, my dear friend Agathon,' Socrates said. 'It's not at all difficult to argue against Socrates.

'Now I'll let you go. I'll try to restate for you the account of Love   d
that I once heard from a woman from Mantinea called Diotima.
She was wise about this and many other things. On one occasion,
she enabled the Athenians to delay the plague for ten years by telling
them what sacrifices to make. She is also the one who taught me
the ways of Love. I'll report what she said, using as a basis the
conclusions I reached with Agathon, but doing it on my own, as far
as I can.[95]

'As you stated, Agathon, one should first describe who Love is
and what his character is and then describe his effects.[96] I think the   e
easiest thing is to report the content of a discussion I once had with
Diotima, in which she put questions to me. I had said to her virtually
the same things that Agathon said to me just now: that Love was a
great god, and that he was himself beautiful.[97] She used against me
the same arguments that I used against him, proving that, according
to my reasoning, Love was neither beautiful nor good.

'I said, "What do you mean, Diotima? Is Love ugly and bad
then?"

'She said, "What blasphemy! Do you think that anything which
isn't beautiful must necessarily be ugly?"

' "I certainly do."   202a

' "And must anything that isn't wise be ignorant? Haven't you
realized that there's something between wisdom and ignorance?"

' "What is it?"

' "It's having right opinions without being able to give reasons
for having them. Don't you realize that this isn't knowing, because
you don't have knowledge unless you can give reasons; but it isn't
ignorance either, because ignorance has no contact with the truth?
Right opinion, of course, has this kind of status, falling between
understanding and ignorance."[98]

' "You're right," I said.

' "Then don't think that what isn't beautiful must be ugly, and   b
that what isn't good must be bad. In the same way, when you
yourself agree that Love is neither good nor beautiful, don't suppose

Love must be described.

that he must therefore be ugly and bad, but something in between these two."

' "But", I said, "it's agreed by everyone that Love is a great god."

' "Do you mean everyone who doesn't know," she asked, "or do you also include those who do?"

' "Absolutely everyone."

'She laughed and said, "But Socrates, how could people agree

c that Love is a great god if they deny he's a god at all?"

' "Who are these people?" I said.

' "You're one," she said, "and I'm another."

'At this I demanded, "How can you say this?"

' "Easily," she said. "Tell me, do you think that all gods are happy and beautiful? Or would you dare to suggest that any of the gods is not beautiful and happy?"[99]

' "By Zeus, I wouldn't," I said.

' "And you call happy those who are in possession of good and beautiful things?"

' "Certainly."

d ' "But you've agreed that it's because Love is in need of good and beautiful things that he desires those very things that he needs."

' "Yes, I've agreed to that."

' "So how could he be a god if he is not in possession of beautiful and good things?"

' "That's impossible, as it seems."

' "Do you see, then," she said, "that you don't believe Love is a god?"

' "But what could Love be?" I said. "A mortal?"

' "Far from it."

' "What then?"

' "Like those examples discussed earlier," she said, "he's between mortal and immortal."

' "What does that make him, Diotima?"

' "He is a great spirit, Socrates. Everything classed as a spirit falls

e between god and human."[100]

Love is encased in all things.

' "What function do they have?" I asked.

' "They interpret and carry messages from humans to gods and from gods to humans. They convey prayers and sacrifices from humans, and commands and gifts in return for sacrifices from gods. Being intermediate between the other two, they fill the gap between them, and enable the universe to form an interconnected whole. They serve as the medium for all divination, for priestly expertise in sacrifice, ritual and spells, and for all prophecy and sorcery. Gods 203a do not make direct contact with humans; they communicate and converse with humans (whether awake or asleep) entirely through the medium of spirits. Someone whose wisdom lies in these areas is a man of the spirit, while wisdom in other areas of expertise and craftmanship makes one merely a mechanic. There are many spirits, of very different types, and one of them is Love."

' "Who are his father and mother?" I asked.

' "That's rather a long story," she replied, "but I'll tell you anyway.   b Following the birth of Aphrodite, the other gods were having a feast, including Resource, the son of Invention. When they'd had dinner, Poverty came to beg, as people do at feasts, and so she was by the gate. Resource was drunk with nectar (this was before wine was discovered), went into the garden of Zeus, and fell into drunken sleep. Poverty formed the plan of relieving her lack of resources by having a child by Resource; she slept with him and became pregnant   c with Love. So the reason Love became a follower and attendant of Aphrodite is because he was conceived on the day of her birth; also he is naturally a lover of beauty and Aphrodite is beautiful.[101]

' "Because he is the son of Resource and Poverty, Love's situation is like this. First of all, he's always poor; far from being sensitive and beautiful, as is commonly supposed, he's tough, with hardened skin, without shoes or home. He always sleeps rough, on the ground,   d with no bed, lying in doorways and by roads in the open air; sharing his mother's nature, he always lives in a state of need. On the other hand, taking after his father, he schemes to get hold of beautiful and good things. He's brave, impetuous and intense; a formidable hunter,

The definition[39] of spirit is necessary.

always weaving tricks; he desires knowledge and is resourceful in getting it; a lifelong lover of wisdom; clever at using magic, drugs and sophistry.[102]

e   ' "By nature he is neither immortal nor mortal. Sometimes on a single day he shoots into life, when he's successful, and then dies, and then (taking after his father) comes back to life again. The resources he obtains keep on draining away, so that Love is neither wholly without resources nor rich. He is also in between wisdom and ignorance. The position is this. None of the gods loves wisdom
204a or has the desire to become wise – because they already are; nor does anyone else who is already wise love wisdom. Nor do the ignorant love wisdom or have the desire to become wise. The problem with the ignorant person is precisely that, despite not being good or intelligent, he regards himself as satisfactory.[103] If someone doesn't think he's in need of something, he can't desire what he doesn't think he needs."

' "Who are the lovers of wisdom, Diotima," I asked, "if they are neither the wise nor the ignorant?"

b   ' "Even a child", she said, "would realize by now that it is those who fall between these two, and that Love is one of them. Wisdom is one of the most beautiful things, and Love is love of beauty. So Love must necessarily be a lover of wisdom; and as a lover of wisdom he falls between wisdom and ignorance.[104] Again the reason for this is his origin: his father is wise and resourceful while his mother has neither quality. So this is the nature of the spirit of Love, my dear
c   Socrates. But it's not at all surprising that you took the view of Love you did. To judge from what you said, I think you saw Love as the object of love instead of the lover: that's why you imagined that Love is totally beautiful. But in fact beauty, elegance, perfection and blessedness are characteristic of the object that deserves to be loved, while the lover has a quite different character, which I have described."[105]

' "Well, Diotima," I said, "I'm sure you're right about this. But if Love is like that, what use is he to human beings?"

Love is wisdom. [40]
Children recognize love.

' "That's the next thing, Socrates," she said; "I'll try to teach you.   d
So far we've dealt with Love's nature and birth; also, according to you,
love is *of* beautiful things. But then, supposing someone asked us,
'*Why* is Love of beautiful things?', or, to put it more clearly, 'The
lover of beautiful things has a desire – what is it that he desires?' "

' "That they become his own," I said.

' "But this answer raises another question," she said. "What will
he get when beautiful things become his own?"

'I said that I didn't have a ready answer to that question.

' "But suppose", she said, "someone changed the question, using   e
the word 'good' instead of 'beautiful',[106] and asked: 'Now then,
Socrates, the lover of good things has a desire – what is it that he
desires?' "

' "That they become his own," I said.

' "And what will he get when good things become his own?"

' "That's easier for me to answer," I said; "he'll be happy."

' "So it's the ownership of good things that makes happy people   205a
happy; and you don't need to ask the further question, 'Why does
someone want to be happy?'[107] This answer seems to mark the end
of the enquiry."

' "That's true," I said.

' "Do you think that this wish and this form of love are common
to all human beings, and that everyone wants good things to be his
own forever,[108] or what is your view?"

' "Just that," I said; "it's common to everyone."

' "In that case, Socrates," she said, "why don't we say that everyone
is a lover, if everyone always loves the same things; why do we call   b
some people lovers and not others?"

' "That's something I've wondered about too," I said.

' "It's nothing to wonder about," she said. "What we're doing is
picking out one kind of love and applying to it the name ('love')
that belongs to the whole class, while we use different names for
other kinds of love."

' "Can you give me another example?" I asked.

Any type of love is consistent

' "Yes, this one. You know that composition forms a general class. When anything comes into being which did not exist before, the

c   cause of this is always composition. So the products of all the crafts are compositions and the craftsmen who make them are all composers?"

' "That's right," I said.

' "But you know that they aren't called composers but have different names. Out of the whole class of composition we pick out one part, the one related to music and verse, and call that by the name of the class as a whole. It's only this that's called composition and those who have this subdivision of the skill are called composers."[109]

' "That's right," I said.

d   ' "The same goes for love. In essence, every type of desire for good things or happiness is what constitutes, in all cases, 'powerful and treacherous love'.[110] But this can be approached by many routes, and those who do so by other means, such as making money or athletics or philosophy, aren't described as 'loving' or 'lovers'. It's only those whose enthusiasm is directed at one specific type who are described by the terminology that belongs to the whole class, that of love, loving and lovers."

' "I suppose that's right," I said.

' "The idea has been put forward", she said, "that lovers are people

e   who are looking for their own other halves. But my view is that love is directed neither at their half nor their whole unless, my friend, that turns out to be good.[111] After all, people are even prepared to have their own feet or hands amputated if they think that those parts of themselves are diseased. I don't think that each of us is attached to his own characteristics, unless you're going to describe the good as 'his own' and as 'what belongs to him', and the bad as 'what does not belong to him'. The point is that the only object of

206a   people's love is the good – don't you agree?"

' "By Zeus, I do!" I said.

' "Well then," she said, "can we quite simply say that people love the good?"

' "Yes," I said.

' "But shouldn't we add," she said, "that the object of their love is that they should have the good?"

' "Yes, we should add that."

' "Not only that," she said, "but that they should have the good forever."

' "We must add that too."

' "To sum up then," she said, "love is the desire to have the good forever."

' "What you say is absolutely right," I said.

' "Given that love always has this overall goal," she said, "we should also ask this. In what way and in what type of action must people pursue this goal, if the enthusiasm and intensity they show in this pursuit is to be called love?[112] What function does love really have: can you tell me?"

' "If I could, Diotima," I said, "I wouldn't be so amazed at your wisdom, and wouldn't keep coming to you as your student to learn these very things."

' "Then I shall tell you," she said. "Love's function is giving birth in beauty both in body and in mind."

' "One would need to be a prophet to interpret what you're saying," I said. "I don't understand it."

' "Well," she said, "I'll explain it more clearly. All human beings are pregnant in body and in mind, and when we reach a degree of adulthood we naturally desire to give birth. We cannot give birth in what is ugly, only in what is beautiful. Yes, sexual intercourse between men and women is a kind of birth.[113] There is something divine in this process; this is how mortal creatures achieve immortality, in pregnancy and giving birth. This cannot occur in a condition of disharmony. The ugly is out of harmony with everything divine, while the beautiful fits in with it. So Beauty is the goddess who, as Fate or Eileithyia, presides over childbirth. That's why, when a pregnant creature comes close to something beautiful, it becomes gentle and joyfully relaxed, and gives birth and reproduces. But

43

when it comes close to something ugly, it frowns and contracts in pain; it turns away and shrivels up and does not reproduce; it holds the foetus inside and is in discomfort. That's why those who are pregnant and already swollen get so excited about beauty:[114] the bearer of beauty enables them to gain release from the pains of childbirth. You see, Socrates," she said, "the object of love is not beauty, as you suppose."

' "What is it then?"

' "Reproduction and birth in beauty."

' "That may well be so," I said.

' "It certainly is," she said. "And why is reproduction the object of love? Because reproduction is the closest mortals can come to being permanently alive and immortal. If what we agreed earlier is right, that the object of love is to have the good *always*, it follows that we must desire immortality along with the good.[115] It follows from this argument that the object of love must be immortality as well."

'Diotima taught me all this in her talks with me about the ways of love. One day she asked, "What do you think, Socrates, is the cause of this love and desire? Haven't you noticed what a terrible state animals of all kinds (footed beasts as well as winged birds) get into when they feel the desire to reproduce. They are all sick with the excitement of love, that makes them first want to have sex with each other and then to rear what they have brought into being. Even the weakest of animals are ready to fight with the strongest and die for the sake of their young; they are prepared to be racked with hunger themselves in order to provide food for their young, and to do anything else for them. Humans, you might think, do this because they understand the reason for it; but, in the case of animals, what causes this excitement of love – can you tell me?"

'I said again that I didn't know.

'She said, "Do you think you'll ever become an expert in the ways of love if you don't understand this?"

' "But that's why I come to study with you, Diotima, as I said

44

Reproduction carries us all.

before, because I realize I need teachers. So tell me the reason for this, and for everything else connected with the ways of love."

' "Well then," she said, "if you believe that the natural object of love is what we've often agreed, you shouldn't be surprised at this. The point made about humans applies also to animals; mortal nature   d does all it can to live forever and to be immortal. It can only do this by reproduction: it always leaves behind another, new generation to replace the old. This point applies even in the period in which each living creature is described as alive and as the same – for instance, someone is said to be the same person from childhood till old age. Although he is called the same person, he never has the same constituents, but is always being renewed in some respects and experiencing loss in others, for instance, his hair, skin, bone, blood and his whole body. This applies not only to the body but also to   e the mind: attributes, character-traits, beliefs, desires, pleasures, pains, fears – none of these ever remain the same in each of us, but some are emerging while others are being lost. Still more remarkable is the fact that our knowledge changes too, some items emerging,   208a while others are lost, so we are not the same person as regards our knowledge; indeed, each individual item of knowledge goes through the same process. What is called studying exists because knowledge goes from us. Forgetting is the departure of knowledge, while study puts back new information in our memory to replace what is lost, and so maintains knowledge so that it seems to be the same.

' "This is the way that every mortal thing is maintained in existence, not by being completely the same, as divine things are, but because everything that grows old and goes away leaves behind another new   b thing of the same type. This is the way, Socrates, that mortal things have a share in immortality, physically and in all other ways; but immortal things do so in a different way.[116] So you shouldn't be surprised if everything naturally values its own offspring. It's to achieve immortality that everything shows this enthusiasm, which is what love is."

'But in fact, when I heard her speech, I was surprised and said,

Our knowledge changes too,

"Well, Diotima, you're very wise, but are things really as you say?"

c   'Like a perfect sophist, she said, "You can be sure about this.[117] You can see the same principle at work if you look at the way people love honour. You'd be amazed at your own stupidity if you failed to see the point of what I've said, after considering how terribly they are affected by love of becoming famous 'and storing up immortal fame for eternity'.[118] They are readier even to risk every

d   danger for this than for their children's sake, and to spend money, suffer any kind of ordeal, and die for honour. Do you think", she said, "that Alcestis would have died for Admetus, or that Achilles would have added his death to that of Patroclus, or that your Athenian hero Codrus would have died to defend his sons' kingdom,[119] if they had not thought that the memory of their courage (which we still hold in respect) would last forever? They certainly wouldn't," she said. "I think it is undying virtue and glorious fame of this sort that motivates everyone in all they do, and the better they are, the

e   more true this is; it's immortality they are in love with.

'"Men who are pregnant in body," she said, "are drawn more towards women; they express their love in trying to obtain for themselves immortality and remembrance and what they take to be happiness forever by producing children. Men who are pregnant in

209a   mind – there are some," she said, "who are even more pregnant in their minds than in their bodies, and are pregnant with what it is suitable for a mind to bear and bring to birth. So what is suitable? Wisdom and other kinds of virtue: these are brought to birth by all the poets and by those craftsmen who are said to be innovative. Much the most important and finest type of wisdom", she said, "is that connected with the organization of cities and households, which is called moderation and justice. Take also the case of someone

b   who's been pregnant in mind with these virtues from a young age. When he's still without a partner and reaches adulthood, he feels the desire to give birth and reproduce. He too, I think, goes around looking for beauty in which to reproduce; he will never do so in ugliness. Because he's pregnant, he's attracted to beautiful bodies rather than ugly ones; and if he's also lucky enough to find a mind that is beautiful, noble and naturally gifted, he is strongly drawn to this combination. With someone like this, he immediately finds he has the resources to talk about virtue and about what a good man should be like and should do, and tries to educate him.

   c

' "It is, I think, when someone has made contact and formed a relationship with beauty of this sort that he gives birth to, and reproduces, the child with which he has long been pregnant. He thinks about the other's beauty, whether they are in each other's company or not, and together with him he shares in bringing up the child reproduced in this way.[120] People like that have a much closer partnership with each other and a stronger bond of friendship than parents have, because the children of their partnership are more beautiful and more immortal. Everyone would prefer to have children like that rather than human ones. People look enviously at

   d

Homer and Hesiod and other good poets, because of the kind of children they have left behind them, which provide them with immortal fame and remembrance by being immortal themselves. Or take," she said, "the children that Lycurgus left in Sparta to provide security to Sparta and, you might say, to Greece as a whole. Solon is also respected by you Athenians for the laws he fathered;[121] and other men, in very different places, in Greece and other countries,

   e

have exhibited many fine achievements and generated virtue of every type. Many cults have been set up to honour these men as a result of children of that kind, but this has never happened as a result of human children.

' "Even you, Socrates, could perhaps be initiated in the rites of love I've described so far. But the purpose of these rites, if they are

  210a

performed correctly, is to reach the final vision of the mysteries; and I'm not sure you could manage this. But I'll tell you about them," she said, "and make every effort in doing so; try to follow, as far as you can.[122]

' "The correct way", she said, "for someone to approach this business is to begin when he's young by being drawn towards

Resources are invaluable.

47

beautiful bodies. At first, if his guide leads him correctly, he should love just one body and in that relationship produce beautiful discourses. Next he should realize that the beauty of any one body is

b closely related to that of another, and that, if he is to pursue beauty of form, it's very foolish not to regard the beauty of all bodies as one and the same. Once he's seen this, he'll become a lover of all beautiful bodies, and will relax his intense passion for just one body, despising this passion and regarding it as petty. After this, he should regard the beauty of minds as more valuable than that of the body, so that, if someone has goodness of mind even if he has little of the

c bloom of beauty, he will be content with him, and will love and care for him, and give birth to the kinds of discourse that help young men to become better. As a result, he will be forced to observe the beauty in practices and laws and to see that every type of beauty is closely related to every other, so that he will regard beauty of body as something petty. After practices, the guide must lead him towards forms of knowledge, so that he sees their beauty too. Looking now

d at beauty in general and not just at individual instances, he will no longer be slavishly attached to the beauty of a boy, or of any particular person at all, or of a specific practice. Instead of this low and small-minded slavery, he will be turned towards the great sea of beauty and gazing on it he'll give birth, through a boundless love of knowledge, to many beautiful and magnificent discourses and ideas. At last, when he has been developed and strengthened in this way, he catches sight of one special type of knowledge, whose object is the kind of beauty I shall now describe.

e ' "Now try", she said, "to concentrate as hard as you can. Anyone who has been educated this far in the ways of love, viewing beautiful things in the right order and way, will now reach the goal of love's ways. He will suddenly catch sight of something amazingly beautiful in its nature; this, Socrates, is the ultimate objective of all the previous

211a efforts. First, this beauty always *is*, and doesn't come into being or cease; it doesn't increase or diminish. Second, it's not beautiful in one respect but ugly in another, or beautiful at one time but not at

48

Beauty is in everything.

another, or beautiful in relation to this but ugly in relation to that; nor beautiful here and ugly there because it is beautiful for some people but ugly for others. Nor will beauty appear to him in the form of a face or hands or any part of the body; or as a specific account or piece of knowledge; or as being anywhere in something else, for instance in a living creature or earth or heaven or anything else. It will appear as in itself and by itself, always single in form; all   b
other beautiful things share its character, but do so in such a way that, when other things come to be or cease, it is not increased or decreased in any way nor does it undergo any change.[123]

' "When someone goes up by these stages, through loving boys in the correct way, and begins to catch sight of that beauty, he has come close to reaching the goal. This is the right method of approaching the ways of love or being led by someone else: beginning   c
from these beautiful things always to go up with the aim of reaching that beauty. Like someone using a staircase, he should go from one to two and from two to all beautiful bodies, and from beautiful bodies to beautiful practices, and from practices to beautiful forms of learning. From forms of learning, he should end up at that form of learning which is of nothing other than *that* beauty itself, so that he can complete the process of learning what beauty really is.

' "In that form of life, my dear Socrates," said the Mantinean   d
stranger, "if in any, human life should be lived, gazing on beauty itself. If you ever saw that, it would seem to be on a different level from gold and clothes and beautiful boys and young men. At present you're so overwhelmed when you see these that you're ready, together with many others, to look at your boyfriends and be with them forever, if that was somehow possible, doing without food and drink and doing nothing but gazing at them and being with them. So what should we imagine it would be like", she said, "if someone could see beauty itself, absolute, pure, unmixed, not   e
cluttered up with human flesh and colours and a great mass of mortal rubbish, but if he could catch sight of divine beauty itself, in its single form? Do you think", she said, "that would be a poor life for

212a a human being, looking in that direction and gazing at that object with the right part of himself[124] and sharing its company? Don't you realize," she said, "that it's only in that kind of life, when someone sees beauty with the part that can see it, that he'll be able to give birth not just to images of virtue (since it's not images he's in touch with), but to true virtue (since it's true beauty he's in touch with). It's someone who's given birth to true virtue and brought it up who has the chance of becoming loved by the gods, and immortal – if any human being can be immortal."[125]

b   'Well, Phaedrus and the rest of you, this is what Diotima said, and I was convinced. Because I was convinced, I try to convince others that, to acquire this possession, you couldn't easily find a better partner for human nature than Love. That's the basis for my claiming that every man should hold Love in respect, and I myself respect the ways of love and practise them with exceptional care. That's why I urge others to do the same, and on this and every other occasion I do all I can to praise the power and courage of Love.[126]

c   So this is my speech, Phaedrus. If you like, you can think of it as a eulogy of Love or if you prefer, you can give it whatever name you like to give it.'[127]

After Socrates' speech, Aristodemus said, while the others congratulated him, Aristophanes was trying to make a point, because Socrates had referred to his speech at some stage. Suddenly, there was a loud noise of knocking at the front door, which sounded like revellers, and they heard the voice of a flute-girl.[128]

d   'Slaves, go and see who it is,' Agathon said. 'If it's any of my friends, invite them in; if not, tell them the symposium's over and we're just now going to bed.'

Not long after, they heard the voice of Alcibiades in the courtyard; he was very drunk and was shouting loudly, asking where Agathon was and demanding to be brought to him. He was brought in, supported by the flute-girl and some of the other people in his

e   group. He stood by the door, wearing a thick garland of ivy and violets, with masses of ribbons trailing over his head, and said:[129]

'Good evening, gentlemen. Will you let someone who's drunk – very drunk – join your symposium? Or should we just put a garland on Agathon, which is why we've come, and go away? I couldn't come to your celebration yesterday,' he said. 'But I've come now with the ribbons on my head, so that I can transfer them directly from my head to that of the man who is – I'd like to announce – the wisest and most beautiful. I suppose you'll laugh at me because I'm drunk. But even if you laugh at me, I know quite well I'm telling the truth. But tell me right away whether 213a I can come in on these terms or not. Can I join you for a drink, or not?'

Everyone shouted out, telling him to come in and take a place on a couch, and Agathon invited him too. So he came in, supported by his friends. He was untying the ribbons to tie them on Agathon, and they fell over his eyes. So he didn't notice Socrates, but sat down next to Agathon, between him and Socrates, who moved   b over when he saw him. When he'd sat down, he embraced Agathon and tied the garland round his head.

Agathon said, 'Take off his sandals, slaves, so that he can lie down and be the third on this couch.'

'Fine,' said Alcibiades; 'but who's this third person drinking with us?' As he said this, he turned round and saw Socrates. When he saw him, he jumped up and said, 'Oh Heracles, what's going on here? Is this Socrates? You've been lying here in wait for me again, so that you can play your usual trick of turning up suddenly wherever   c I least expect you. Why have you come here? And why did you choose this couch? I see you didn't pick Aristophanes or anyone else who's prepared to make a fool of himself, but you made sure you'd be lying beside the most attractive man in the room.'

Socrates said, 'Agathon, please protect me. What a nuisance my love for this man has become! Ever since I started loving him, I haven't been able to look at or talk to a single attractive man without   d his getting so jealous and resentful that he goes crazy and shouts at me and almost beats me up. So make sure that he doesn't do anything to me now and make peace between us; or if he starts to get violent, protect me from him. I'm quite terrified by his mad attachment to his lovers.'[130]

'There can be no peace between me and you,' Alcibiades said. 'I'll get my own back on you for this another time. But for now, Agathon,' he said, 'give me back some of those ribbons, so that I can tie them on this amazing head of his. Otherwise, he'll criticize me for tying them on your head, not his, even though he *always* beats off all comers in verbal contest – and you've just done it once, two days ago.'[131]

As he spoke, he took some of the ribbons, and tied them on Socrates, and lay down again. When he settled down, he said, 'Well, gentlemen, you look sober to me. This can't be allowed; you have to drink. This was what we agreed. For our master of ceremonies, to take charge of the drinking, until you're drunk enough, I elect – myself! Have a big goblet brought in, Agathon, if you've got one. Or rather, there's no need; bring me, boy, that wine-cooler,' he said, seeing one that held more than four pints. He had this filled up, and drank it down himself, and then he told the slave to fill it up for Socrates. As he did so, he said, 'Not that my trick will have any effect on Socrates, gentlemen. However much you tell him to drink, he drinks without ever getting more drunk.'[132]

The slave filled it for Socrates and, while he was drinking it, Eryximachus said, 'What sort of behaviour is this, Alcibiades? Aren't we going to have any conversation or songs as we pass round the cup, but do nothing but drink as though we were thirsty?'

Alcibiades said, 'Hello, Eryximachus, best of sons of the best – and most temperate – of fathers.'

'Hello to you too,' Eryximachus said; 'but what should we do?'

'Whatever you tell us. We should obey you, because "a doctor is equal in worth to many other men";[133] so tell us to do whatever you want.'

'Listen to me then,' Eryximachus said. 'Before you arrived, we'd decided to take turns, going round from left to right, making the

Drinking solves spirits

finest speech each of us could, in praise of Love. All the rest of us c have given our speeches. You haven't taken your turn at speaking, though you've done well at drinking, so it's right for you to make a speech. Once you've spoken, you can order Socrates to do whatever you want, and he can do the same to the person on his right and so on.'

'That's a good idea, Eryximachus,' Alcibiades said. 'But I don't think it's fair to make someone who's drunk compete against speeches made by people when they were sober. Also, my dear friend, I hope you don't believe any of what Socrates just said. Don't you realize d that the truth is quite the opposite of what he said? If I praise anyone else, whether god or human, while he's around, it's he who'll beat *me* up.'

'What blasphemy!' Socrates said.

'By Poseidon!' Alcibiades said, 'don't contradict me on this point. I'm never going to praise anyone else while you're around.'

'Well then, do just that, if you want,' Eryximachus said. 'Give a eulogy of Socrates.'[134]

'What do you mean?' said Alcibiades. 'Do you think I should, e Eryximachus? Should I attack him and punish him in front of you all?'

'Hang on,' said Socrates. 'What are you planning – to give a eulogy that makes fun of me, or what?'

'I'll tell the truth – will you let me do that?'

'But of course I'll let you tell the truth; indeed, I order you to.'

'Here I go then,' Alcibiades said. 'But this is what you can do. If I say anything that isn't true, interrupt, if you like, and point out that what I'm saying is false. I don't want to say anything that's false. But if I don't remember things in the right order, don't be surprised. 215a It isn't easy for someone in my condition to list all the aspects of your peculiarity in a fluent and orderly sequence.[135]

'The way I'll try to praise Socrates, gentlemen, is through images. Perhaps he'll think this is to make fun of him; but the image will be designed to bring out the truth not to make fun. My claim is that

Company generates.
conditions are relevant.

b   he's just like those statues of Silenus you see sitting in sculptors' shops. The figures are produced holding shepherd's pipes or flutes;[136] when they're opened up, you find they've got statues of the gods inside. I also claim he's like Marsyas the satyr. Not even you, Socrates, could deny that you resemble these in appearance; but you're going to hear next how you're like them in other ways too.[137]

'You're insulting and abusive, aren't you?[138] If you don't admit this, I'll provide witnesses. And aren't you a flute-player? In fact, you're a much more amazing one than Marsyas. He used instruments

c   to bewitch people with the power of his mouth, and so does anyone who plays his flute-music today. (I'm counting the tunes of Olympus as really Marsyas', because Marsyas was Olympus' teacher.)[139] Whether these tunes are played by an expert player or a poor flute-girl, they're the only ones which, because of their divine origin, can cast a spell over people and so show which ones are ready for the gods and initiation into the mysteries.[140] The only difference between you and Marsyas is that you produce this same effect without

d   the use of instruments, by words alone. Whenever we hear someone else making speeches, even if he's a very good orator, this has virtually no impact on any of us. But whenever anyone hears you speak or hears your words reported by someone else (even if he's a very poor speaker), whoever we are – woman, man or boy – we're overwhelmed and spellbound.

'If it weren't for the fact that you'd think I was completely drunk, gentlemen, I'd take an oath on the truth of what I'm saying about the effect his words have had on me – an effect they still have now.

e   Whenever I listen to him, my frenzy is greater than that of the Corybantes. My heart pounds and tears flood out when he speaks, and I see that many other people are affected in the same way. I've heard Pericles and other good orators, and I thought they spoke well. But they haven't produced this kind of effect on me; they haven't disturbed my whole personality and made me dissatisfied

216a   with the slavish quality of my life.[141] But this Marsyas here has often had this effect on me, and made me think that the life I'm leading

Instruments are
necessary.

isn't worth living. You can't say this isn't true, Socrates. Even now I'm well aware that if I allowed myself to listen to him I couldn't resist but would have the same experience again. He makes me admit that, in spite of my great defects, I neglect myself and instead get involved in Athenian politics. So I force myself to block my ears and go away, like someone escaping from the Sirens, to prevent myself sitting there beside him till I grow old.[142]

'He's the only person in whose company I've had an experience   b you might think me incapable of – feeling shame with someone; I only feel shame in his company. I'm well aware that I can't argue against him and that I should do what he tells me; but when I leave him, I'm carried away by the people's admiration. So I act like a runaway slave and escape from him; and whenever I see him, I'm ashamed because of what he's made me agree to. Often I've felt I'd be glad to see him removed from the human race; but if this did   c happen, I know well I'd be much more upset. I just don't know how to deal with this person.

'This is the effect this satyr has had on me and many other people with his flute-playing. Listen to other ways that he's like these creatures I'm comparing him with and what amazing power he has. You should realize that none of you really knows him. But I'll show what he's like, now that I've made a start. You see that Socrates is   d erotically attracted to beautiful boys, and is always hanging around them in a state of excitement. Also he's completely ignorant and knows nothing. In giving this impression, isn't he like Silenus? Very much so. This behaviour is just his outer covering, like that of the statues of Silenus.[143] But if you could open him up and look inside, you can't imagine, my fellow-drinkers, how full of moderation he is! You should know that he doesn't care at all if someone is beautiful – he regards this with unbelievable contempt – or is rich or has any   e of the other advantages prized by ordinary people. He regards all these possessions as worthless and regards us as worth nothing too (believe me!). He spends his whole life pretending[144] and playing with people.

'I don't know if any of you have seen the statues inside Socrates
when he's serious and is opened up. But I saw them once, and they
217a   seemed to me so divine, golden, so utterly beautiful and amazing,
that – to put it briefly – I had to do whatever Socrates told me to.
I thought he was seriously interested in my looks and that this was
a godsend and an amazing piece of good luck, because, if I gratified
him, I'd be able to hear everything he knew. You see, I was incredibly
proud of my good looks. Before this, I had never been alone with
him without an attendant; but once I'd got this idea I sent the
b   attendant away and was with him on my own. Yes, I must tell you
the whole truth; so pay careful attention, and, if I say anything that's
not right, Socrates, you must contradict me.

'Well, there we were, gentlemen, the two of us on our own. I
thought he would immediately have the kind of conversation with
me that lovers have with their boyfriends when they're on their
own, and I was pleased by that thought. But nothing like that
happened at all. He had his usual kind of conversation with me and
went away after spending the day with me. After that I invited him
c   to come to the gymnasium with me and we exercised together; I
thought I would get somewhere that way. So we exercised together
and wrestled on many occasions with no one around – and what
can I tell you? I got nowhere.[145]

'Since I was getting nowhere by these means, I decided to make
a direct assault on the man, and not to give up now that I'd made a
start. I felt I had to know how things stood. I invited him to dinner,
just as though I were the lover and he the boy I had designs on. He
d   wasn't quick to accept my invitation, but eventually agreed to come.
The first time he came, he wanted to go after dinner, and on that
occasion I was ashamed and let him go. But I continued my plan
another time, and when we'd had dinner I kept the conversation
going far into the night. Then, when he wanted to go, I made the
excuse that it was too late to go, and made him stay. So he settled
down to sleep on the couch next to mine, where he'd had dinner,
and there was no one else sleeping in the room but us.

'Up to this point, it would have been all right for anyone to hear   e
what I've said. But from now on there are things you wouldn't have
heard me say except that, as the saying goes, "there's truth in wine
when the slaves have left", and when they haven't![146] Also, I think
it would be wrong of me to let Socrates' proud action pass into
oblivion now that I've embarked on his eulogy. Besides, my experience is that of someone bitten by a snake. They say that someone
who's had this experience is only prepared to say what it's like to
those who've been bitten themselves, because they're the only ones
who'll understand and make allowances if the pain drives you to do   218a
and say shocking things. I've been bitten by something more painful
still, and in the place where a bite is most painful – the heart or
mind, or whatever you should call it. I've been struck and bitten by
the words of philosophy, which cling on more fiercely than a snake
when they take hold of a young and talented mind, and make
someone do and say all sorts of things. Also I can see here people
like Phaedrus, Agathon, Eryximachus, Pausanias, Aristodemus and   b
Aristophanes – I don't need to mention Socrates himself – and the
rest of you. You've all shared the madness and Bacchic frenzy of
philosophy, and so you will all hear what I have to say. You will all
make allowances for what I did then and what I'm saying now. But
you, house-slaves, and any other crude uninitiates, put big doors on
your ears![147]

'So, gentlemen, when the lamp was out and the slaves had left
the room, I decided I shouldn't beat about the bush but tell him   c
openly what I had in mind. I gave him a push and said, "Socrates,
are you asleep?"

'"Not at all," he said.

'"Do you know what I've been thinking?"

'"What exactly?" he said.

'"I think", I said, "you're the only lover I've ever had who's
good enough for me, but you seem to be too shy to talk about it to
me. I'll tell you how I feel about this. I think I'd be very foolish not
to gratify you in this or in anything else you need from my property

Philosophy has truth

d   or my friends. Nothing is more important to me than becoming as good a person as possible, and I don't think anyone can help me more effectively than you can in reaching this aim. I'd be far more ashamed of what sensible people would think if I failed to gratify someone like you than of what ordinary, foolish people would think if I did."[148]

'He listened to what I said, and then he said this, in a highly ironic manner and one that was entirely typical of him: "My dear Alcibiades, it looks as though you're really no fool, if what you say about me e   is true and I somehow do have the capacity to make you a better person. You must be seeing in me a beauty beyond comparison and one that's far superior to your own good looks. If you've seen this and are trying to strike a deal with me in which we exchange one type of beauty for another, you're planning to make a good profit from me. You're trying to get true beauty in return for its appearance, 219a   and so to make an exchange that is really 'gold for bronze'.[149] But look more closely, my good friend, and make sure you're not making a mistake in thinking I'm of value to you. The mind's sight begins to see sharply when eyesight declines, and you're a long way from that point."

'When I heard this, I said, "As far as I'm concerned, this is the position, and my plans are exactly as I've said. It's now up to you to consider what you think is best for you and for me."

' "Well," he said, "you're right about that at least. In the future b   we'll consider and do whatever seems best to us, both in this and in other things too."

'When he made this reply to what I'd said, now that I'd fired my shots, I thought he'd been wounded. I got up from my couch, and without letting him say anything more I wrapped him in my thick outdoor cloak (it was winter then) and lay down under his short cloak.[150] Then I threw my arms round this really god-like[151] and c   amazing man, and lay there with him all night long. And you can't say this is a lie, Socrates. After I'd done all this, he completely triumphed over my good looks – and despised, scorned and insulted them – although I placed a very high value on these looks, gentlemen of the jury. I'm calling you that because you've become the jury in the case of Socrates' arrogance! I swear to you by the gods, and by the goddesses, that when I got up next morning I had no more *slept with* Socrates than if I'd been sleeping with my father or elder brother.   d

'After that, what state of mind do you think I was in? Although I felt I'd been humiliated, I admired his character, his self-control and courage. Here was someone with a degree of understanding and tough-mindedness I'd never expected to find. So, although I couldn't be angry with him or do without his company, I didn't know how to win him over. I knew well that he was more completely   e invulnerable to the power of money than Ajax was to weapons;[152] and what I'd seen as the only means of catching him had proved a failure. I was baffled; and I went around more completely enslaved to this person than anyone else has ever been to anyone.

'It was after these events had occurred that we served together in the Athenian campaign against Potidaea and shared the same mess there.[153] The first thing to note is that he put up with the rigours of warfare better than me – better than everyone else, in fact. When we were cut off, and forced to do without food, as sometimes happens on campaign, no one came near him in putting up with   220a this. But on the other hand when we had a feast, he was best able to enjoy it. For instance, though reluctant to drink, when he was forced to, he beat us all at it. The most amazing thing of all is that no one has ever seen Socrates drunk. I think you'll see proof of this shortly.[154]

'Also when it came to putting up with winter (the winters there are terrible), his endurance was remarkable. On one occasion there was such a bitter frost that no one went outside, or if they did, they   b wrapped themselves up with clothes in the most amazing way and tied on extra pieces of felt or sheepskin over their boots. But Socrates went out in this weather wearing the same outdoor cloak he'd usually worn before, and he made better progress over the ice in his

bare feet than the rest of us did in boots. The soldiers regarded him
c   with suspicion, thinking that he was looking down on them.

'So much for that incident; but "what the stout-hearted man did
and endured next"[155] on campaign there is well worth hearing.
One morning he started thinking about a problem and stood there
considering it, and when he didn't make progress with it he didn't
give up but kept standing there examining it. When it got to midday,
people noticed him and said to each other in amazement that Socrates
had been standing there thinking about something since dawn. In
the end, when it was evening, some of the Ionians,[156] after they'd
d   had dinner, brought their bedding outside (it was summer then),
partly to sleep in the cool, and partly to keep an eye on Socrates to
see if he would go on standing there through the night too. He
stood there till it was dawn and the sun came up; then he greeted
the sun with a prayer and went away.

'If you'd like to know what he was like in battle – here it's right
for me to repay a debt to him. During the battle after which the
generals awarded me the prize for bravery, it was Socrates, no one
e   else, who rescued me. He wasn't prepared to leave me when I was
wounded and so he saved my life as well as my armour and weapons.
I actually told the generals to award the prize for bravery on that
occasion to you, Socrates. This is a point on which you can't criticize
me or say that I'm lying. But when the generals wanted to award
the prize to me, influenced by my social status, you yourself were
keener than the generals that I should receive it.

'Here's another thing, gentlemen. Socrates was a sight worth
221a   seeing when the army made a disorderly retreat from Delium. It
turned out that I was serving in the cavalry there while he was a
hoplite. People had scattered by then in all directions, and he was
retreating together with Laches. As it happened, I was near by, and
when I saw them I encouraged them at once, and told them I
wouldn't leave them behind. I was better able to watch Socrates
there than at Potidaea (because I was on horseback I was less worried

about my safety), and the first thing that struck me was how much more self-possessed he was than Laches. Next, I noticed that he was walking along there, just as he does here in Athens – to use your phrase, Aristophanes – "swaggering and looking from side to side". He was calmly looking out both for friends and enemies, and it was obvious to everyone even from a long distance that if anyone tackled this man, he would put up a tough resistance.[157] That was how he and his companion got safely away. Generally, people don't tackle those who show this kind of attitude in combat; they prefer to chase those who are in headlong flight.

'There are many other remarkable things which you could say in praise of Socrates. Some of these distinctive features could perhaps also be attributed to other people too. But what is most amazing about him is that he is like no other human being, either of the past or the present. If you wanted to say what Achilles was like, you could compare him with Brasidas or others, and in Pericles' case you could compare him with Nestor or Antenor[158] (and there are other possibilities), and you could draw other comparisons in the same way. But this person is so peculiar, and so is the way he talks, that however hard you look you'll never find anyone close to him either from the present or the past. The best you can do is what I did, in fact, when I compared him, and his way of talking, not with human beings but with Sileni and satyrs.

'This is something I forgot to say at the beginning: his discussions are also very like those Sileni that you open up. If you're prepared to listen to Socrates' discussions, they seem absolutely ridiculous at first. This is because of the words and phrases he uses, which are like the rough skin of an insulting satyr. He talks about pack-asses, blacksmiths, shoemakers and tanners, and seems to be always using the same words to make the same points; and so anyone unused to him or unintelligent would find his arguments ridiculous. But if you can open them up and see inside, you'll find they're the only ones that make any sense. You'll also find they're the most divine and contain the most images of virtue. They range over most – or rather all – of the subjects that you must examine if you're going to become a good person.[159]

'This is what I have to say, gentlemen, in praise of Socrates. I've also mixed in some blame as well, and told you how he insulted me.

b I'm not the only one he's done this to; there's also Charmides the son of Glaucon, Euthydemus the son of Diocles and many others.[160] He deceives them into thinking he's their lover and then turns out to be the loved one instead of the lover. I'm warning you, Agathon, not to be deceived by him, but to learn from what we've suffered and be cautious, and don't, as the proverb puts it, be the fool who only learns by his own suffering.'

c This speech of Alcibiades created much amusement at his frankness, because he seemed to be still in love with Socrates. Socrates said, 'I think you're sober after all, Alcibiades. Otherwise you wouldn't have been able to conceal the motive of your entire speech by ingeniously disguising it in this way. You slipped it in at the end as though it was an afterthought – as though the point of the whole

d speech hadn't been to make trouble between myself and Agathon. You did this because you think that I should love you and no one else, and that Agathon should be loved by you and no one else. But you haven't got away with it; we've seen the purpose of this satyr-play – and Silenus-play – of yours.[161] But, my dear Agathon, don't let him succeed in this; make sure that no one comes between me and you.'

Then Agathon said, 'You know, Socrates, I think you must be

e right. It's significant that he lay down in the middle, between me and you, to keep us apart. But he won't succeed in doing this. I'll come round and lie down beside you.'

'Please do,' said Socrates; 'come here and lie down on the other side.'

'Oh Zeus!' said Alcibiades, 'what I suffer from this person! He thinks he always has to get the better of me. But if nothing else – you amazing man – let Agathon lie down between us.'

Don't be a fool.
Get the better of others.

'But that's impossible,' Socrates said. 'You've praised me, and now it's my turn to praise the one on my right. If Agathon lies down between us, won't he too have to praise me, instead of being praised by me? For goodness' sake, don't stop the young man from being praised by me; I feel a strong desire to give his eulogy.' 223a

'Hurrah!' said Agathon. 'Alcibiades, there's no way I'm going to stay here now. I simply must change positions and be praised by Socrates.'

'Here we go again,' said Alcibiades; 'it's always the same. When Socrates is around, no one else can get a look-in with the attractive men. Now, too, see how resourcefully he's found a plausible reason why this one should lie down beside him.'[162]

So Agathon got up to go and lie down beside Socrates. Suddenly, b a large group of revellers came to the front door. They found it open because someone was just going out; so they marched straight in to join them, and settled themselves down on the couches. There was noise everywhere, and all order was abandoned; everyone was forced to drink vast amounts of wine. Aristodemus said that Eryximachus and Phaedrus and some of the others went off then, while he fell asleep for a very long time, because the nights were long at c that time of year. He woke up when it was nearly dawn and the cocks were already crowing. Once he'd woken up, he saw that the others were either asleep or had left, and that Agathon, Aristophanes and Socrates were the only ones still awake, drinking from a large bowl that they passed from left to right. Socrates was engaged in dialogue with them. Aristodemus said he couldn't remember most d of the argument, because he'd missed the start and was half-asleep anyway. But the key point, he said, was that Socrates was pressing them to agree that the same man should be capable of writing both comedy and tragedy, and that anyone who is an expert in writing tragedy must also be an expert in writing comedy. He was getting them to agree this, though they were sleepy and not following very well; Aristophanes fell asleep first, and Agathon feel asleep when day was already breaking.

63

Praise others.
Get people to agree w/ you

After getting them off to sleep, Socrates got up and went off. Aristodemus followed him as usual. Socrates went to the Lyceum, had a wash, spent the rest of the day as he did at other times, and only then in the evening went home to bed.[163]

Get people to agree with you.

NOTES

1. The *Symposium* begins with a frame-conversation which stresses two main points: the eagerness of several people to find out about the speeches on love at a famous symposium and the enthusiasm with which certain people (including Aristodemus and Apollodorus) follow Socrates in adopting philosophy as a way of life. Both are indications of the 'erotic' power of the search for truth; see Introduction, xviii–xix.

2. The playfulness seems to lie in the urgency with which the other person stops Apollodorus to make what is (by normal standards) a non-urgent request: getting a report of a much earlier social event. Another possible explanation is that the opening address, 'the man from Phalerum', uses a formal style playfully in an informal context. Phalerum is a port town just east of Peiraeus in Attica.

3. This Phoenix is not known otherwise.

4. A Glaucon (Plato's half-brother) is a main interlocutor in Plato's *Republic* and another is mentioned, as father of Charmides (who is Plato's uncle), in Plato, *Charmides* 154b and *Symposium* (*Symp.*) 222b. It is not clear which Glaucon is meant here.

5. Agathon left Athens for the court of Archelaus of Macedon at some date before 405 BC. Nussbaum (1986), 168–71, suggests that readers are meant to think that this conversation occurred in 404, just before Alcibiades' death, when the question of Alcibiades' return from exile was a current issue. Alcibiades is mentioned in 172b; on the significance of the date of the symposium (416) for Alcibades' life, see n. 135.

6. Tragedies were performed, normally only once, in competition with each other at one of Athens' major religious festivals each year. To win the competition, as Agathon first did at the Lenaean festival early in 416 BC, was a major public achievement (see also 175e).

7. Aristodemus is not otherwise well known; he appears as Socrates' follower in Xenophon, *Memorabilia* 1.4. He is identified by his district or 'deme', as was normal in Classical Athens. In not wearing shoes or sandals, he copies Socrates (174a, 220b). On 'love' (not necessarily sexual) in Socrates' social circles, see Introduction, xv; Aristodemus exemplifies the 'erotic' pull of the philosophical search for truth (see n. 1).

8. The city is Athens; on the philosophical significance of journeys (in pursuit of the truth) in this Platonic dialogue and others, see Osborne (1994), 86–90.

9. There is a pointed contrast between 'softy' and Apollodorus' 'savage' criticisms of other ways of life; Apollodorus' 'soft' character is shown in Plato, *Phaedo* 117d, in his emotional response to Socrates' imminent execution. There is an alternative textual reading, 'mad' or 'maniac'.

10. The fact that Socrates was normally barefoot and did not take full-scale baths (just a simple wash, 223d) shows the simplicity and toughness of his way of life, stressed by Alcibiades (219e–220b).

11. 'Good-looking' or 'beautiful' (*kalos*). Agathon's good looks are also mentioned in 213c. He is the 'boyfriend' in his relationship with Pausanias (193b–c), and is in his mid-thirties in 416 BC; see Introduction, n. 49 above. In Aristophanes' *Thesmophoriazusae* 29–35 (411 BC), he is presented as effeminate; perhaps he shaved his beard close to look like a young man.

12. The version of the proverb that is 'proved wrong' is 'Good men go uninvited to inferior men's banquets'. The variation Socrates gives (which is also found elsewhere) includes a pun, since in Greek 'good men's' (*agathôn*) is the same as 'Agathon'.

13. Menelaus is described as a 'soft spearman' in Homer, *Iliad* 17.587–8; Menelaus goes uninvited to Agamemnon's feast in 2.408.

14. An inaccurate quotation of Homer, *Iliad* 10.224, which is quoted more accurately in Plato, *Protagoras* 348d.

15. Sharing a couch to recline on was normal at a Greek symposium; on the arrangements at a symposium, see Introduction, xi–xii.

16. For this as a habit of Socrates', see also 220c–d. More stressed elsewhere is his habit of virtually continuous dialectic (see 194c–e, 199b–201c and Introduction, xvi); presumably, his private reflection is an internalized version of this dialectic. Here, Socrates' behaviour shows his indifference to social convention (despite 174a), by contrast with his total commitment to philosophical search for the truth.

17. Here and elsewhere (e.g. 174e), Agathon is a very suave host; the implication here is that his household slaves are so good that he doesn't need to keep supervising them.

18. Socrates is referring to Agathon's victory as a tragic poet (n. 6); the number 30,000 is an exaggeration, but the theatre of Dionysus may have held between 10,000 and 20,000. Here and in 194b, Socrates is, by implication, sceptical about the value of the public display of 'wisdom' in the form of tragic drama; on Plato's generally low estimate of poetic wisdom, see Introduction, xxvi. For a similarly sarcastic comment by Socrates (to Alcibiades) about contrasting types of beauty (real and apparent), see 218e.

19. Agathon picks up Socrates' sarcastic tone: he accuses him of *hubris*, 'contempt' or even 'violence'. Agathon apparently refers to Dionysus as the god of wine and thus patron of the symposium; perhaps he also has in mind Dionysus' role as patron of the dramatic festival where Agathon has just been victorious. Later, Agathon admits he is defeated by Socrates in argument (201c); and Alcibiades, entering the symposium like an image of Dionysus, 212e, crowns Socrates as superior in wisdom to Agathon (213e).

20. On the symposium as a highly ritualized, communal event, involving agreement about the quantity and strength of the wine drunk, see Introduction, xi–xiii.

21. See also 214a, 220a, 223c–d; Socrates' imperviousness to drink seems to be presented as part of his exceptional toughness and invulnerability to weakness, emotion or desire.

22. This pompous statement of the obvious is typical of the characterization of Eryximachus in *Symp.*; see Introduction, xxiii. Eryximachus appears as a representative of the medical profession, which was emerging as a branch of expertise at this date; Eryximachus is also shown in Socratic circles in Plato, *Protagoras* 315c.

23. As noted in Introduction, xii–xiii, this proposal indicates that this symposium will be exceptionally intellectual, and also one focused on homo-erotic love.

24. The full line from this (lost) play is 'Not mine the story, but it comes from my mother'.

25. 'Sophist', originally used in Greek to signify anyone with special expertise, came in the late fifth century BC to refer to itinerant intellectuals and teachers, especially of rhetoric. Plato generally presents them very negatively and contrasts them sharply with Socrates, though here he makes Phaedrus, as reported by Eryximachus, speak approvingly about at least some of them ('our best sophists'). Prodicus of Ceos, known especially for his study of language, wrote an allegory about the hero Heracles choosing the hard road of Virtue over the easy road of Vice (Xenophon, *Memorabilia* 2.1.21–34).

26. The power of sexual desire (*erôs*) had been celebrated in, for instance, earlier Greek lyric and tragic poetry; and there were hymns (e.g. the Homeric Hymn) to Aphrodite as goddess of love. But Eros, the male god of love, had not acquired a strongly defined character in mythology or art at this date, though he did so in later antiquity. Though Eros was worshipped in cult, his worship was much less important than that of Aphrodite. See article on 'Eros' in Hornblower and Spawforth (1996); Ferrari (1992), 248–9.

27. Phaedrus is also presented in Plato, *Phaedrus* 228b as a passionate enthusiast for speeches, especially speeches about love (*erôs*).

28. On Socrates' (complex) attitude towards (homo-erotic) love, see Introduction, xxxvii–xxxviii. For Pausanias and Agathon as lover and boyfriend, see 193b–c, also Introduction, n. 49 above. Wine (Dionysus, also the god of drama) and sex (Aphrodite) are central themes in Aristophanic comedy.

29. Hesiod, *Theogony* is an important source of mythology for the Greeks; the lines cited are 116–17 and the start of 120 (omitting 118–19). Acusilaus was a fifth-century collector of myths whose works are lost. Parmenides (fifth-century philosopher), fragment 13 in Diels–Kranz (the standard collection of pre-Socratic philosophers): 'she' may be the goddess Necessity. Phaedrus is selective in his quotations. This idea of Eros is different from much other early Greek poetry and art in which Eros simply embodies sexual power and is sometimes pictured as a young man or boy; see n. 26.

30. In fact, the Thebans set up in 379/8 BC a 'Sacred Band' of homosexual lovers (150 pairs). Since Phaedrus seems to refer to a purely hypothetical idea, *Symp.* is usually dated earlier than this; see Dover (1980), 10.

31. This expression is common in Homeric battle-scenes; see e.g. *Iliad* 10.482, 15.262.

32. On this generalization and the question whether it is consistent with Phaedrus' examples, see Introduction, xxi.

33. Apollo, reciprocating a favour, gave Admetus the chance of avoiding death if someone was willing to die for him; only his wife Alcestis would do so. In Euripides' *Alcestis*, she is brought back to life by Heracles, who wrestles with Death for her.

34. Orpheus was a musician of legendary skill, who used this power to enter the underworld to reclaim his dead wife. Phaedrus' version of the myth is unknown elsewhere. In earlier versions, Orpheus is killed by Maenads (followers of Dionysus). In Virgil, *Georgics* 4.453–527, Orpheus failed to bring Eurydice from the Underworld because he broke the condition that he should not turn round to see her following him.

35. For Achilles' willingness to die to avenge Patroclus, see *Iliad* 18.88–96 (taken in Plato, *Apology* 28c–d as a supreme act of courage), cf. 9.410–16. For Achilles as younger than Patroclus, and the most beautiful of the heroes, see *Iliad* 11.786–7, 2.673–4. In Homer, Patroclus and Achilles are not lovers, but they were in Aeschylus' lost play *Myrmidons*. The islands of the blessed (like Elysium) were sometimes presented in early Greek poetry as the home of dead heroes.

36. Pausanias here draws on two mythological versions of the origin of Aphrodite (from Zeus and Dione, Homer, *Iliad* 5.370–71; from Uranus, Hesiod, *Theogony* 188–206). The two titles 'Heavenly' (Uranian) and 'Common' (*pandêmos*) were also attached to Aphrodite in Greek religion; the latter probably meant 'worshipped by all the people'. But the meaning Pausanias gives to these features is quite new. Uranian Aphrodite is selected for homosexual love perhaps because in Hesiod's version Aphrodite had no mother (she was born from Uranus' castrated genitals) and because she was 'older' (from an older generation of gods) and therefore had more prestige.

37. On the social practices (especially the fact that women received little education in Classical Athens) underlying this view regarding women and sexuality, see Introduction, xiii–xv.

38. 'Abusive violence' is *hubris*, which often means 'rape' in connection with sex but is here used more broadly.

39. This emphasis on lifelong homosexual partnerships is unusual and seems to reflect Pausanias' own well-known partnership with Agathon (see Introduction, n. 49 above). But there are some other parallels (e.g. in Aristophanes' speech, 192b and Plato, *Phaedrus* 256a–e), so it seems to be an available social ideal.

40. Xenophon, *Constitution of Sparta* 2.12–14, provides evidence for a distinction between acceptable (morally educative) and unacceptable homosexual relations similar to that offered by Pausanias in 184c–185b.

41. At the time of the dramatic date of *Symp.* (416 BC), the Greek cities of Ionia were free, though they were under the domination of Persia after 387/6 BC, when *Symp.* was probably being written.

42. In 514 BC Harmodius and Aristogiton tried to kill Hippias, tyrant of Athens, and killed his brother Hipparchus from personal motives, according to Thucydides 6.54–9. But the tyranny fell three years later, and the lovers earned a popular reputation as tyrannicides. In line with typical Greek attitudes (Introduction, xiii–xv), the lover is presented as motivated by desire (*erós*), the boyfriend by 'reciprocal affection' or 'friendship' (*philia*).

43. Plato may wish us to see Pausanias as overstating Athenian willingness to condone male–male love. See Introduction, xxi–xxii; also xxxi–xxxiii on the Socratic–Platonic rejection of the sexual dimension of such relationships. However, Pausanias' speech may be historically accurate in presenting sexual relations between free males in Athens as a peculiarly problematic area, in which the social status of those involved carried both special prestige and special risk.

44. Homer, *Iliad* 2.71.

45. As noted in Introduction, xxii, Plato makes Pausanias, here and in 185b, stress only the boyfriend's concern with moral self-improvement, while the lover's concern is directed at the (sexual) gratification he obtains from the relationship; note especially 'the lover is justified . . . the boyfriend who gratifies him'. Given that the relationship is commended because of its morally educative aim (185b, cf. 181c–d), you might expect the lover too to have this as his primary aim. There is a pointed contrast with 209b–c, 210b–c, which stresses the lover's concern with the other's education and which removes any reference to sexual gratification.

46. See n. 45. Note especially 'keen to do anything for anybody' (185b), referring to the boyfriend's gratification of the lover. Here, the lover *is* presented as 'paying attention' to virtue, but to *his own*, presumably so that he can become a 'good man' (185a) and so win the boyfriend's co-operation. Note also that the relationship 'forces' (*anangkazôn*) him to do this, by contrast with the more spontaneous production of virtue (in the lover and perhaps the loved one) in the ideal of Socrates–Diotima (212a).

47. 'Word-play' is, literally, 'speaking in equal units': 'Pausanias' and 'came to a pause' (*pausamenou*) have the same number and length of syllables as well as echoing each other. The implication is that Pausanias' speech shows the influence of sophists, teachers of rhetoric (cf. Plato, *Protagoras* 315d–e, where Pausanias is presented as a pupil of Prodicus; note also the rhetorical word-play of Agathon's speech, esp. 197c–e). It may also be implied that the speech is rhetorically skilful advocacy of a form of love which Plato wants us to see as inferior (nn. 45–6).

48. Eryximachus, like his father Acumenus, is mentioned as a doctor by Xenophon and Plato; Eryximachus also appears in Plato, *Protagoras* 315c. The name suggests 'belch-fighter' in Greek, a point which ties in neatly with his attempts to cure Aristophanes' hiccups. He appears here as a representative of medicine and is presented rather satirically (Introduction, xxiii).

49. The significance of the hiccups has been much debated by scholars; the most obvious point (explicit in 189a) is that their 'disorderly' character and cure undermines Eryximachus' claim that medicine restores bodily 'order' (but see n. 57). Ferrari (1992), 250, suggests that the shift in order of speeches gives added emphasis to Aristophanes' more profound speech.

50. For Pausanias' point, see 184c–185c; for the (rather awkward) shift in standpoint here, see Introduction, xxii–xxiii.

51. For medicine as a science of 'filling and emptying', cf. Hippocrates, *On Humours* 1, and *On Regimen in Health* 1. See also n. 57.

52. On this second theme in Eryximachus' speech and its relationship to the first (in 186b–c), see Introduction, xxii–xxiii.

53. Asclepius is the legendary founder of medicine, and appears as this in Homer and Hesiod (i.e. in 'poets like those here', Aristophanes and Agathon).

54. This fragment of the philosopher Heraclitus (sixth–fifth century BC) is given in various forms; it is 51 in Diels–Kranz. Despite his subsequent pompous correction of Heraclitus, Eryximachus seems completely to miss Heraclitus' point, as modern scholars understand this. This is that the universe ('unity' or 'the one') consists of a tension between coexisting opposites, and that musical harmony exhibits the same tension. See e.g. Kahn (1979), 195–200, who numbers the fragment as 78.

55. The awkwardness with which Eryximachus combines his two themes (Introduction, xxii–xxiii) is especially marked in this part of his speech.

56. Both the Heavenly Muse (Urania) and Polymnia appear in Hesiod's list of Muses (*Theogony* 75–9), though they are not given specific functions; Eryximachus picks these two names out as the nearest to Pausanias' types of love (180d–e). The idea that music can affect emotion and shape ethical character is prominent in Greek thought, e.g. Plato, *Republic* 397–400, *Laws* 799–802.

57. Aristophanes' comment, though clearly intended as a joke, may bear out Eryximachus' idea that medicine is the science of 'filling and emptying' (186c): the sneeze empties the excess air in the hiccup. However, his comment also captures our sense that Eryximachus' picture of the world, and his attempt to impose 'order' on his subject, is not wholly successful.

58. Aristophanes (*c. 450–c.* 385 BC) was the most famous Athenian comedian in the late fifth and early fourth century, and a number of his comedies survive. His *Clouds* (423 BC) is a powerful, though inaccurate, attack on Socrates (in Plato, *Apology* 18b–19c, Plato's Socrates describes it as an influential one), but there is little sign of bitterness between the two men here. This speech is not very like Aristophanic comedy, except in being amusing and having a strong, vivid theme. It is more like an intellectual's version of a myth or Aesopic fable (see e.g. Protagoras' myth in Plato, *Protagoras* 320d–322d); see also Dover (1966), (1980), 112–13.

59. In fact, there *was* a cult of Eros at this date, but a minor one; see n. 26.

60. 'Androgynous' was used to mean an effeminate or cowardly man. The idea of combining the functions of the two genders (e.g. male 'pregnancy') also occurs in Socrates' speech, 206c–e, 208e–209c.

61. The idea of the sun as male, 'Mother' earth as female, and the moon as bisexual has some parallels in Greek thought.

62. Ephialtes and Otus were huge humans who planned to overthrow the gods by piling mountains on each other and were destroyed by Apollo, Zeus' son (Homer, *Odyssey* 11.307–20).

63. Cicadas actually mate normally (though their young fall to the ground, where they live underground prior to adulthood); but some grasshoppers lay eggs directly on the ground, and Plato may be thinking of these.

64. Aristophanes suggests that flatfish look like full-bodied fish cut in half; a 'matching half' or 'tally' (*sumbolon*) is an object cut in half to serve as a recognition-token.

65. Adulterers and adulteresses are given as exemplars of heterosexual love because marriage (often arranged) was not standardly seen in Classical Athens as a context for the kind of passionate or romantic love that is the subject here (see Introduction, xiv–xv). This is the only passage from Classical Athens recognizing the existence of female homosexuality; the term is *hetairistriai* (cf. *hetairai*, 'female companions'), not lesbians, a modern usage based on the passionate love poetry to women by Sappho of Lesbos.

66. This is a joke, based on the familiar comic taunt (alluded to in Aristophanes, *Clouds* 1093–4) that politicians were (passive) homosexual partners in their youth as a way of advancing their careers. There may also be some parody of Pausanias' claim that maleness is shown by being attracted to men (181c). But the joke reflects the likelihood (Introduction, xv) that the all-male contexts of Greek high-status activities, including politics, promoted homo-erotic relations between men.

67. The scene probably echoes the Homeric one in which Hephaestus, the blacksmith god, traps the two lovers, Aphrodite (his wife) and Ares, caught in the act of love-making, and calls the other gods to see them (Homer, *Odyssey* 8.266–366); but here Hephaestus' offer to 'unite' the two lovers is more positive. Agathon alludes to the Ares–Aphrodite affair in 196d.

68. For this type of redefinition of what 'love' means, see Socrates–Diotima in 205d–e, alluding to Aristophanes' theory, but only to contradict it. On the importance of the Hephaestus-scene for understanding the significance of Aristophanes' speech, see Introduction, xxv.

69. This is almost certainly an (anachronistic) allusion to the Spartan division of the city of Mantinea into four separate settlements in 385 BC; see Mattingly (1958), Dover (1965).

70. Dice were used as 'matching halves' or 'tallies' (n. 64).

71. See nn. 28 and 39.

72. The exchange takes up the issue raised in 175d–e (n. 18) about the relationship between public and private wisdom. Agathon tries to parry Socrates' scepticism about publicly displayed wisdom but is pursued in Socrates' characteristic style of dialectic until Phaedrus intervenes (194d).

73. Agathon, the most famous Athenian tragedian after Aeschylus, Sophocles and Euripides, was well known for his elaborate, rhetorical style, his effeminacy (both parodied in Aristophanes, *Thesmophoriazusae* 30–172, presented in 411 BC), and his sexual partnership with Pausanias (nn. 28 and 39). Born sometime after 450, he must have been in his mid-30s in 416. On the general character of his speech, see Introduction, xxv–xxvi. The claim to be giving a proper definition of the subject recurs throughout *Symp.* (see 180c–e, 186a–b, here at 195a, 198d–199c, 205a–206b). But this self-consciously methodical style is also characteristic of Gorgias; see n. 87.

74. As noted earlier (n. 26), Eros did not have a fixed image at this date, but he was sometimes pictured as a beautiful young man (rather than the chubby child of later antiquity). Agathon is contradicting Phaedrus' picture of Eros as among the oldest of the gods (178a–c), though without providing quotations from earlier poets to support this.

75. Cronus was son of Uranus and Iapetus was his brother; they are stock examples of antiquity (Phaedrus does not use these examples).

76. In Hesiod's *Theogony*, there is much mutual violence between gods (e.g. Cronus castrates his father Uranus) before the present world-order is established; we have nothing of this type in our surviving fragments of Parmenides, though we find reference to a goddess Necessity.

77. *Iliad* 19.92–3 (part of a famous description of Delusion, *Atê*, by Agamemnon).

78. The link between Eros and flowers is traditional in Greek poetry, though Agathon's main interest here is in linking Eros with the 'bloom' of youth (*anthos*, 'flower' also suggests youthful 'bloom').

79. Agathon ascribes the four 'cardinal virtues' (justice, courage, moderation, wisdom) to Love, and each one is ascribed with playful use of fallacy, another characteristic of Gorgias' rhetoric. Here the point is that because Love never 'forces' (or is 'forced'), he is never unjust (taken to be identical with using force). The final quotation is attributed by Aristotle to the fourth-century orator Alcidamas.

80. The fallacy here lies in equivocating between 'mastering' (i.e. controlling) pleasures and desires and 'mastering' (i.e. exceeding) one desire by a stronger one. The virtue is *sôphrosunê*, also translated as 'self-control' or 'temperance'. For a more serious argument about the meaning of 'mastering' desires and pleasures (and being 'mastered' by them), see Plato, *Protagoras* 353c–357e.

81. Since the god of war was 'captured' (in love) by Aphrodite (a further reference to the Ares–Aphrodite affair, cf. n. 67), Love is braver than the bravest – a completely illogical conclusion.

82. Euripides fragment 663 (*Stheneboea*); Eryximachus referred to his expertise in 186b. The final extravagant claim about virtue is that, because Love inspires people to poetry, and poetry is identical with wisdom, Love is wise.

83. Developing the previous claim about Love and wisdom, Agathon suggests that, because all innovations are motivated by desire (i.e. the desire to innovate), Love is an innovator.

84. Agathon presents his string of fallacies as supporting his earlier assertion (195c) that Love's dominance established the present world-order, which was itself a piece of creative mythology. Agathon shifts at this point from claiming that Love is beautiful (195a–b) to claiming that love is *of beauty*, a shift picked up in Socrates' subsequent argument (200e–201b); see Ferrari (1992), 252.

85. We do not know whether these lines are quoted from a lost play by Agathon or have been made up by Plato, presumably in the style of Agathon.

86. This remarkable passage seems to combine parody of the elaborate style of the orator Gorgias (on whom see n. 87) and of Agathon himself, whose poetic style is satirized in Aristophanes, *Thesmophoriazusae* 101–29. Features obvious even in translation include short and symmetrically balanced clauses (isocolon), threefold repetition (tricolon), absence of connectives (asyndeton), rhyme and assonance. Also the thirty-one phrases (or cola) are all in recognizable Greek verse metres; see Dover (1980), 123–4.

87. Socrates, heavy-handedly, spells out the influence of Gorgias on Agathon's speech with a Homeric allusion (taken from *Odyssey* 11.633–5) to the head of the Gorgon Medusa which turns people to stone. Gorgias of Leontini (*c*. 485–*c*. 380 BC) was an influential orator and sophist in the late fifth and early fourth centuries. His speeches exhibited features evident in Agathon's speech, including extravagant claims, strained reasoning and ornate poetic prose. Other features reminiscent of Gorgias are the self-conscious methodology (194e–195a), the listing of points and the providing of 'evidence' for each claim (196d–e).

88. An allusion to a notorious line (Euripides, *Hippolytus* 612), also used satirically in Aristophanes, *Frogs* 1471.

89. The dialogue 199d–201c is a typical piece of Socratic dialogue in that Socrates uses directed questions to show the interlocutor that he holds inconsistent beliefs, and leads him to abandon his original claim. The argument is focused on the sense of *erôs* as 'desire', rather than (interpersonal) 'love' in the conventional sense (see Introduction, xi and xxviii).

90. The aim of Socratic dialectic is not just to consider beliefs in isolation but to examine their logical implications, that is to see what *necessarily* follows from holding a particular belief; Socrates underlines this point here.

91. It is natural to take 'he' as 'the lover'; but 'he' could also be taken to mean 'Love'. This ambiguity is taken further in 201b (see n. 93). The two points referred to were agreed in 199e, 200e.

92. See 197b and n. 84.

93. This inference is questionable. Socrates seems to move from the idea that *the lover* needs and lacks beauty (the subject, translated 'he' in 201b, is unspecified, cf. 200e and n. 91) to the idea that *Love* needs and lacks beauty. (The *experience* of love might be beautiful even if the lover desires and 'needs' someone beautiful.) His next move (also questionable) is to assume that something that 'needs' beauty is 'wholly without beauty'.

94. *Kalos* in Greek has a broad range of meanings; translated 'beautiful' here, it can also mean 'fine, right, noble' and, when it does, is close in meaning to 'good' (*agathos*), which can mean 'morally good' or 'beneficial'. The suggestion here seems to be that 'good things' form a subdivision of 'beautiful things', not that the two classes are identical. But see also 204e–205a (with n. 106), where the two classes seem to be treated as identical. The introduction of 'good' is especially relevant to the argument with Agathon because he had claimed that Love possessed the virtues (i.e. was good) as well as being beautiful.

95. On Diotima and her significance, see Introduction, xxviii–xxix. Although she continues to argue through leading questions, and shows up her interlocutor's inconsistencies (e.g. 202c–d), her tone is much more dogmatic and authoritative than Socrates'. The idea that the Athenians had reason, in 440 BC, to fear the plague which actually occurred in 430 BC is not supported by any other evidence.

96. See 194e and n. 73.

97. '. . . he was himself beautiful': the Greek is more ambiguous, 'he was *of* beautiful things' or 'he was *one of* the beautiful things'. Agathon claimed both: the first in 197b, cf. 201a, the second in 195a, 197c. But it was the latter claim (that Love was beautiful) that is argued against in 201b, cf. later in 201e, and the translation reflects this.

98. In this passage, wisdom (*sophia*), knowledge (*epistêmê*) and understanding (*phronêsis*) are used as synonyms, contrasted with right opinion by the ability to give reasons. For this way of distinguishing knowledge and right opinion, see Plato, *Meno* 97a–99a, *Theaetetus* 201d–210a; also Annas (1981), ch. 8, Fine (1992).

99. In Greek mythology gods are not always beautiful or happy; but Diotima presumes the kind of philosophically revised theology (e.g. Plato, *Republic* 379–83) in which gods have all good qualities. On what 'happiness' means in Greek thought, see n. 107.

100. 'Spirit' is *daimôn*, sometimes treated in earlier Greek as a synonym for 'god', sometimes (as here) as a lower order of being; the idea of *daimones* as intermediaries was developed in later antiquity by Plutarch and Plotinus. The role of 'spirits' as links between mortal and immortal prepares us for the role of love in this respect (207a); see also Osborne (1994), 108–13.

101. Like Aristophanes' speech, this is a myth invented to make a point: that love combines a state of need with the means to satisfy this need. For selective or partly inventive uses of Greek myths about Love see 178a–b, 180d–e, 187d–e, 195b–c (also n. 58).

102. Several features in this description (e.g. 'tough, with hardened skin, without shoes . . . a lifelong lover of wisdom') evoke Socrates, especially as described later by Alcibiades. See 174a and 219e–220d; Osborne (1994), 93–101. The allusion serves to associate love with one specific type of search, the philosophical search for truth, as symbolized by Socrates; see 204a–b and Introduction, xxix.

103. A recurrent theme of Socratic dialectic in the early Platonic dialogues is trying to show people that they are ignorant about what they think they understand (e.g. the nature of virtue) and that they need to engage in philosophy, which is the search for understanding about such things.

104. Love is here identified with one specific type of 'intermediate' state (202a–203a) and one type of search to satisfy a need, namely the search for wisdom. The identification of love with philosophy helps to explain Socrates' claim to expertise in the ways of love (177d, 199b, also *Lysis* 204b–c). The definition of love is later made much more general (205a–206a), though the philosophical search for truth is presented as an ideal form of love in Diotima's mysteries (210d–212a).

105. Socrates–Diotima returns to the feature of Agathon's speech on which the argument has focused since 200a (see 195a, 197c, also the characterization in 197d, esp. 'elegance'). On the significance of identifying 'love' with 'the lover', see Introduction, xxviii–xxix.

106. Diotima talks here as if she is asking a different question, but the identification of love (i.e. desire for beautiful things) with the desire for good things in 205a implies that good things are identical with beautiful things. Analogously, the Form of Beauty (in 210e–212a) plays the same role as the Form of Good plays in Plato, *Republic*, 505a–509c. See Dover (1980), 144; Kahn (1996), 267–71.

107. 'Happiness' (*eudaimonia*) is standardly seen as the overall goal of human life in Greek thought, and as an objective condition not a subjective feeling. Associated in conventional Greek thought with achievement, prosperity and family well-being, it is often identified by Greek philosophers with virtue. The term 'ownership' should not be taken to mean that this theory of love is egoistic; the relevant kind of 'ownership' (gaining 'immortality along with the good') is later shown to be a form of procreation or reproduction, in a way that benefits others; see 206e–207a, also Osborne (1994), 54–7, 102–3.

108. The addition 'forever', emphasized at 206a, though introduced without separate argument, plays a key role in the rest of Diotima's theory.

109. The Greek term translated 'composition' is *poiêsis*, which means both 'making' or 'creation' in general and, specifically, 'poetry'. 'Composition' is given here as an English term with comparable broad and specific meanings: since 'poetry' in Greek included setting words for music (e.g. in tragedy), (musical) 'composition' is quite close in meaning to Greek 'poetry'.

110. This seems to be a quotation; the source is unknown.

111. A clear reference back to Aristophanes' speech (and a rejection of its central idea), as Aristophanes sees (212c).

112. Here Diotima uses the general motive identified as 'love' in 205a–206a to explain the subdivision of this motive (marked by a special 'enthusiasm and intensity') that is normally called 'love'.

113. Diotima here underlines the radical modification of concepts of gender and sexuality that goes along with her revision of what 'love' means; see Introduction, xxxi–xxxii, also 206d and 208e–209e.

114. The language recalls both male and female reactions. 'Relaxed' suggests female reactions in sexual intercourse and the dilation of the cervix in childbirth. 'Contracts', 'shrivels' suggest the contraction of the cervix (cf. 'holds the foetus inside') and the shrinking of the penis. 'Swollen' suggests both female labour and male erection.

115. Diotima refers back to 205a, 206a; there 'forever' (or 'always', *aei*) could have been taken just to mean 'throughout one's life', but here the claim is that 'always' involves the idea of immortality. The idea that 'reproduction and birth *in beauty*' (206e) gives permanent possession of the *good* seems to depend on taking 'beauty' and 'good' to be identical; see n. 106. For the claim that sexual intercourse (here, in animals as well as humans, 207b–c) has an underlying motive of which those involved are not aware, cf. Aristophanes' speech (192c–e).

116. There is no explicit reference in *Symp.* to the idea of the immortality of the soul or mind that is prominent elsewhere in Plato, e.g. *Phaedo*, though that may be implied in 212a (see n. 125). The stress falls on immortalization through reproduction; the application of this idea to human minds as well as bodies in 207d–208a strikingly anticipates some modern thinking about personal identity. See Price (1989), 30−35, on Parfit's theory and on Platonic thinking in general about immortality.

117. Diotima is like a 'perfect sophist' (probably ironic, in view of Plato's general scepticism about sophists) because of her authoritative and dogmatic tone, by contrast with the Socratic stance of 'knowing nothing'. See also 204a−b, 206b, 207c; Introduction, xvii, xxviii−xxix.

118. Hexameter verse quotation: source unknown.

119. Codrus was a mythical king of Attica who gave his life to save his city from Dorian invaders (Diotima of Mantinea speaks as a non-Athenian). The other examples are taken from Phaedrus' speech (179b−180b): Diotima is, in effect, correcting Phaedrus by offering a more profound explanation for such acts.

120. On the language of female reproduction used to describe the male−male erotic-educational relationship, see 206c−d and Introduction, xxxi−xxxii. The contrast between attraction to bodies and to minds recalls Pausanias in 181b. But this version of the erotic-educational relationship stresses the features noted as missing in Pausanias' speech, i.e. positive interest in the boyfriend's ethical education (their 'child') and absence of sexual desire (see Introduction, xxii).

121. Lycurgus was a semi-legendary figure who founded the distinctive Spartan constitution and so helped Sparta play a crucial role in the Persian Wars (thus providing 'security . . . to Greece as a whole'). Solon reshaped the Athenian constitution in the early sixth century BC, and Athenian laws were called 'the laws of Solon'. On the question whether this extension of the idea of immortality through reproduction fits Diotima's pattern (is the beauty in which birth occurs that of the community?), see Price (1989), 27−8.

122. On the mysteries of Diotima and the issues they raise, see Introduction, xxxii−xxxv. In Greek, the rest of 210a−d (i.e. the next paragraph in translation) forms one extended sentence, spelling out the stages of the ascent. For a comparable 'ascent', see the movement out of the cave to the Form of the Good in Plato, *Republic* 514−17; cf. also the beneficial outcome of both ascents for other people (*Republic* 519c−520d, *Symp.* 212a−b).

123. This characterization of the Form of Beauty (or 'the beautiful', *kalon*) includes the four features singled out as characteristic of Forms in Irwin (1989), 90−91 (a helpful short account of the theory). These are: (1) unchanging stability of character; (2) freedom from the simultaneous presence of opposites; (3) being known by the mind not by the senses; (4)

separation from those perceptible things which share the character of the Form. The last feature is stressed also in 211d–e. See also Introduction, xxxiii.

124. That is the rational mind, when properly prepared to understand the Form; cf. Plato, *Republic* 490b, 518c–519b.

125. The outcome of the ascent is here linked with Diotima's overall account of the aim of love, gaining 'immortality along with the good' through '[r]eproduction and birth in beauty' (206e–207a). The 'virtue' produced in this way may be within the character of the lover, of the boyfriend (if he is still in view, cf. 'loving boys' in 211b), or of those influenced by the lover who has completed the ascent (212b). Here alone, Diotima seems to envisage immortality of the mind or soul as well as immortality through the 'children' created (here, the virtue). See further Price (1989), 49–54. As elsewhere, such immortality is the result of an extended process of 'purification' from the body; it is also the result of understanding a Form whose character is permanent or eternal (see Introduction, n. 65; and n. 123 above).

126. Socrates' eagerness to urge others to make the ascent of love suggests that the effect of carrying out this ascent (or even of just discovering what it involves) is to make you want to benefit others by urging them to do so; Socrates seems here to take on the role of the guide in the mysteries. See Introduction, xxxiv.

127. Socrates here acknowledges how radically he has enlarged or revised the conventional meaning of 'love'.

128. Alcibiades' arrival marks a sharp contrast to the order of the symposium and the profundity of the previous speech (see Introduction, xiii and xxxv). The word 'suddenly' (*exaiphnes*) is used to mark a significant transition (see also 210e and 213b–c). 'Revellers' are members of a *kômos*, a more disorderly, mobile symposium or street-party.

129. On Alcibiades, see n. 135. As well as being garlanded for a symposium, Alcibiades (very drunk, beautiful and decorated with ivy) appears as an image of the god Dionysus: see n. 131.

130. On this exchange, in which Socrates is described by Alcibiades and himself as a homo-erotic 'lover', in the conventional sense, see Introduction, xxxvii–xxxviii.

131. Agathon's prophecy that his wisdom and that of Socrates will be 'judged' by Dionysus is fulfilled here (taking Alcibiades as 'Dionysus', n.

129); but again (as in 201c), Socrates emerges as the winner. See n. 19; also Bacon (1959).

132. See also 176c, 220a, 223c–d.

133. Homer, *Iliad* 11.514. The exchange between Eryximachus and Alcibiades reflects Eryximachus' earlier role as director of the symposium (and as a doctor all too ready to give advice), 176b–e. However, in the face of Alcibiades' anarchic style, Eryximachus' readiness to impose order is useful.

134. By becoming the subject of Alcibiades' eulogy (instead of Love), Socrates, here and in Diotima's myth (203c–d, n. 102), becomes the supreme exemplar of love.

135. Alcibiades (452–404 BC), a famous Athenian politician, was 36 in 416 BC (about the same age as Agathon). The timing of the symposium is significant; it comes just before a series of highly controversial events: Alcibiades' advocacy of the Sicilian expedition (which finally proved disastrous); the accusation that he had profaned the mysteries of Eleusis and mutilated the Herms (phallic statues of Hermes) in Athens; his association with Sparta and Persia, Athens' enemies, before a brief period (407) when he was again an Athenian general and leader. The stress on the idea that Socrates had tried (but failed) to get Alcibiades to give up politics until he had become, through philosophy, a better person (216a–c) is thus crucial to the defensive presentation of Socrates. The allusions in Alcibiades' speech to statues (cf. Herms) and to mysteries are sometimes taken to allude to these features of Alcibiades' later life; see e.g. 215a–c, 218b; also Nussbaum (1986), 171. On the speech as a whole, see Introduction, xxxv–xxxviii.

136. Though conventionally translated as 'flute', the *aulos* was a double-reeded instrument like a modern oboe.

137. The satyrs (led by Silenus) had snub noses and bulging eyes, as did Socrates (cf. Plato, *Theaetetus* 143e). No Silenus-statues of the type described are known from elsewhere; they seem to be opened by taking them apart like 'Chinese boxes' or possibly on a hinge. On ancient statues of Socrates, in which he is shown as satyr-like, see Zanker (1995), 32–40.

138. *Hubristês*, one who commits assault (including rape) or similar insult. Satyrs (depicted with huge erections pursuing Nymphs) were associated with rape. Socrates, accused of *hubris* ('insult') by Alcibiades in 219c and 222a (cf. Agathon's accusation in 175e), turns out to be guilty of the opposite fault – *failing* to take up the offer of sexual gratification.

139. Both Marsyas and Olympus were traditionally held to have invented the flute (*aulos*).

140. The use of emotionally powerful music (associated with the names of Olympus or the Corybantes, 215e) was a key element in mystery religions. See e.g. Plato, *Ion* 534, *Minos* 318b; Aristotle, *Politics* 1340a8–12; also Dodds (1951), 77–80.

141. On the erotic pull of Socrates (as an exemplar of the search for truth), see Introduction, xviii–xix, and nn. 1 and 7. Apart from Pericles' huge reputation as an orator, this comment takes on added point from the fact that Pericles brought up Alcibiades after the death of his father; by implication Pericles, as well as Socrates, has failed to help Alcibiades develop into a good person.

142. For Socrates' theme that 'the unexamined life is not worth living', see Plato, *Apology* 38a; on the conflict between the claims of politics and philosophy, see e.g. Plato, *Gorgias* 484d–488a.

143. See 215a–b and nn. 137–8. Silenus is characterized by drunkenness, ignorance and sexual lust. For Socrates as 'knowing nothing', see Introduction, xvi, and on Socrates' apparent homo-eroticism, see Introduction, xxxvii–xxxviii.

144. 'Pretending' is *eirôneuomenos*, or 'being ironic' (cf. 218d); on Socratic 'irony' as pretended ignorance, see Vlastos (1991), ch. 1.

145. Wrestling (done naked in Classical Athens) gave obvious opportunities for homosexual advances.

146. Alcibiades seems to be citing (and then adapting) a proverb about the frankness of drunken men when unobserved by slaves. There is no known parallel to this proverb, though there is a related one: 'wine and boys [or "slaves", *paides*] tell the truth'.

147. The reference to the mysteries (cf. 215c and n. 135), in preparation for Alcibiades' revelation of the truth about Socrates, marks this passage as the equivalent of Diotima's mysteries (cf. esp. 209e–210a).

148. The echo of Pausanias' picture of the lover–boyfriend exchange (esp. 184d, see n. 45) is significant for Alcibiades' erotic assumptions; see Introduction, xxxvi–xxxvii.

149. A reference to Homer, *Iliad* 6.232–6, where Glaucus foolishly gives golden armour in return for bronze; here, the unequal exchange is moral or mental beauty (virtue) in return for the sexual gratification of enjoying physical beauty.

150. Socrates' 'short cloak' is a *tribôn*, normally for summer use only; Alcibiades' 'thick outdoor cloak' is a *himation* for winter use (which even Socrates wore in the extreme conditions mentioned in 220a–b). Both men probably also wore underclothes as was normal at night.

151. 'God-like' is *daimonios*, confirming the echoes of Socrates in the description of the *daimôn* or 'spirit' of Love (203c–d).

152. In Homer's *Iliad*, Ajax was famously hard to wound because of his fighting ability and large shield.

153. The city of Potidaea was besieged by Athens for two years at the start of the Peloponnesian War (432–430 BC).

154. On Socrates' imperviousness to drink, see n. 21.

155. Homer, *Odyssey* 4.242 and 271, slightly modified.

156. These took part in the campaign as Athenian allies.

157. The Athenian army was routed by the Boeotians on its return from setting up a garrison at Delium in Boeotia in 424 BC. Laches, a well-known Athenian general, is presented in Plato, *Laches* 181b, as impressed by Socrates' courage in battle. The Aristophanes quotation is from *Clouds* 362 (modified).

158. Brasidas, a Spartan general of great skill and courage (died 422 BC), is compared to the most renowned warrior in Homer's *Iliad*. Pericles, the famous fifth-century politician and orator, is compared to Nestor and Antenor, noted in Homer's *Iliad* for wisdom and skill in oratory.

159. For Silenus-statues and the insulting satyr Marsyas, see 215a–b; for divine statues, see 216e–217a. On Socratic dialectic, see Introduction, xvi. The reference to 'pack-asses, blacksmiths' etc. is to Socrates' repeated comparison of moral and intellectual excellence to skills or crafts; see e.g. Plato, *Gorgias* 490a–491b.

160. Charmides, Plato's uncle and a right-wing politician; in Plato, *Charmides* 155d–e, Socrates presents himself as sexually excited by him. Euthydemus, a good-looking young man mentioned in Xenophon, *Memorabilia* esp. 1.2.29, 4.2.1 (not the sophist who is the main interlocutor in Plato, *Euthydemus*).

161. A satyr-play (semi-comic and featuring a chorus of satyrs and Silenus) followed each set of tragedies in the dramatic festivals (for Silenus and satyrs see 215a–c). By implication, Alcibiades' speech is the satyr-play after the more serious ('tragic') speeches. For *Symp.* as a philosophical equivalent of tragedy and comedy, see Introduction, xxxix, referring to 223d.

162. On Socrates' readiness to play the game of homo-erotic relationships (despite Alcibiades' disclosure of his lack of sexual responsiveness), see Introduction, xxxvii–xxxviii. The word 'resourcefully' (*euporôs*) echoes the idea of Love as child of Resource (*Poros*), 203b–c, confirming the assimilation of Socrates to Love in 203c–d (see n. 102).

163. On the significance of the two closing incidents, see Introduction, xxxix. The Lyceum was a gymnasium and public baths.

SELECT BIBLIOGRAPHY

This bibliography contains all the works referred to (by author and date) in the Introduction and Notes, together with a selection of recent works in English on the *Symposium*. Books cited in incomplete form, e.g. Kraut (1992), are identified fully elsewhere in this bibliography.

Symposium: Greek texts with introductions and commentaries

Bury, R. G., ed., *The Symposium of Plato* (2nd edn, Cambridge, 1932).
Dover, K. J., ed., *Plato: Symposium* (Cambridge, 1980).
Rowe, C. J., ed., *Plato: Symposium* (Warminster, 1998); also contains a translation.

Symposium: Translations with introductions and notes

Allen, R. E., in *The Dialogues of Plato*, vol. 2 (New Haven, Conn., 1991).
Cobb, W. S., *The Symposium and the Phaedrus: Plato's Erotic Dialogues* (Albany, NY, 1993).
Nehamas, A. and Woodruff, P., *Plato: Symposium* (Indianapolis, 1989).
Waterfield, R., *Plato: Symposium* (Oxford, 1994).

Symposium: Discussions

Armstrong, A. H., 'Platonic Eros and Christian Agape', *Downside Review* 79 (1960), 105–21.
Bacon, H., 'Socrates Crowned', *Virginia Quarterly Review* 35 (1959), 415–30.
Chen, L. C. H., 'Knowledge of Beauty in Plato's *Symposium*', *Classical Quarterly* 33 (1983), 66–74.

Clay, D., 'The Tragic and Comic Poet of the *Symposium*', *Arion* NS 2 (1975), 238–61.

Cornford, F. M., 'The Doctrine of Eros in Plato's *Symposium*', in F. M. Cornford, *The Unwritten Philosophy and Other Essays* (Cambridge, 1950), 68–80; reprinted in Vlastos (1971), 119–31.

Cummings, P. W., 'Eros as Procreation in Beauty', *Apeiron* 10.2 (1976), 23–8.

Dorter, K., 'The Significance of the Speeches in Plato's *Symposium*', *Philosophy and Rhetoric* 2 (1969), 215–34.

Dover, K. J., 'Eros and Nomos (Plato, *Symposium* 182a–185c)', *Bulletin of the Institute of Classical Studies* 11 (1964), 31–42.

——'The Date of Plato's *Symposium*', *Phronesis* 10 (1965), 2–20.

——'Aristophanes' Speech in Plato's *Symposium*', *Journal of Hellenic Studies* 86 (1966), 41–50.

Edelstein, L., 'The Role of Eryximachus in Plato's *Symposium*', *Transactions of the American Philological Association* 75 (1945), 83–103; reprinted in L. Edelstein, *Ancient Medicine* (Baltimore, 1971), 153–71.

Ferrari, G. R. F., 'Platonic Love', in Kraut (1992), 248–76.

Frede, D., 'Out of the Cave: What Socrates Learned from Diotima', in R. M. Rosen and J. Farrell, eds, *Nomodeiktes: Greek Studies in Honor of Martin Ostwald* (Michigan, 1993), 397–422.

Gagarin, M., 'Socrates' Hybris and Alcibiades' Failure', *Phoenix* 31 (1977), 22–37.

Gill, C., 'Platonic Love and Individuality', in Loizou and Lesser (1990), 69–88.

——*Personality in Greek Epic, Tragedy, and Philosophy: The Self in Dialogue* (Oxford, 1996), esp. 383–91.

Gould, T., *Platonic Love* (London, 1963).

Guthrie (1975), 365–96.

Hackforth, R., 'Immortality in Plato's *Symposium*', *Classical Review* 64 (1950), 43–5.

Halperin, D. M., 'Platonic Eros and What Men Call Love', *Ancient Philosophy* 5 (1985), 161–204.

——'Plato and Erotic Reciprocity', *Classical Antiquity* 5 (1986), 60–80.

——'Why is Diotima a Woman? Platonic *Erôs* and the Figuration of Gender', in Halperin, Winkler and Zeitlin (1990), 257–308; also in Halperin (1990), 113–51.

——'Plato and the Erotics of Narrativity', in Klagge and Smith (1992), 93–129.

Konstan, D. and Young-Bruehl, E., 'Eryximachus' Speech in the *Symposium*', *Apeiron* 16 (1982), 40–46.

Kosman, A., 'Platonic Love', in Werkmeister (1976), 53–69.

Levy, D., 'The Definition of Love in Plato's *Symposium*', *Journal of the History of Ideas* 40 (1979), 285–91.

Markus, R. A., 'The Dialectic of Eros in Plato's *Symposium*', *Downside Review* 73 (1955), 219–30; reprinted in Vlastos (1971), 132–43.

Mattingly, H. B., 'The Date of Plato's *Symposium*', *Phronesis* 3 (1958), 31–9.

Moravcsik, J. M. E., 'Reason and Eros in the "Ascent"-Passage of the *Symposium*', in Anton and Kustas (1971), 285–302.

Nussbaum, M. C., 'The Speech of Alcibiades: A Reading of Plato's *Symposium*', *Philosophy and Literature* 3 (1979), 131–72; reprinted in Nussbaum (1986), 165–99.

——*The Fragility of Goodness: Luck and Ethics in Greek Tragedy and Philosophy* (Cambridge, 1986), esp. 165–99.

Osborne, C., *Eros Unveiled: Plato and the God of Love* (Oxford, 1994).

Patterson, R., 'The Platonic Art of Comedy and Tragedy', *Philosophy and Literature* 6 (1982), 76–92.

——'The Ascent in Plato's *Symposium*', *Proceedings of the Boston Area Colloquium in Ancient Philosophy* 7 (1991), 193–214.

Pender, E., 'Spiritual Pregnancy in Plato's *Symposium*', *Classical Quarterly* 42 (1992), 72–86.

Price, A. W., 'Loving Persons Platonically', *Phronesis* 26 (1981), 25–34.

——*Love and Friendship in Plato and Aristotle* (Oxford, 1989), esp. 15–54.

——'Martha Nussbaum's *Symposium*', *Ancient Philosophy* 11 (1991), 285–99.

Santas, G. X., *Plato and Freud: Two Theories of Love* (Oxford, 1988), esp. 14–57.

Sheffield, F., 'Psychic Pregnancy and Platonic Epistemology', *Oxford Studies in Ancient Philosophy* 20 (2001), 1–33.

Stannard, J., 'Socratic Eros and Platonic Dialectic', *Phronesis* 4 (1959), 120–34.

Stokes, M. C., *Plato's Socratic Conversations: Drama and Dialectic in Three Dialogues* (London, 1986), ch. 3.

Vlastos, G., 'The Individual as an Object of Love in Plato', in Vlastos (1981), 3–42.

White, F. C., 'Love and Beauty in Plato's *Symposium*', *Journal of Hellenic Studies* 109 (1989), 149–57.

Wolz, H. G., 'Philosophy as Drama: An Approach to Plato's *Symposium*', *Philosophy and Phenomenological Research* 30 (1969–70), 323–53.

Socrates and Plato

Annas, J., *An Introduction to Plato's Republic* (Oxford, 1981).

——'Plato', in Hornblower and Spawforth (1996), 1190–93.

Anton, J. P. and Kustas, G. L., eds, *Essays in Ancient Greek Philosophy* (Albany, NY, 1971).

Benson, H. H., ed., *Essays on the Philosophy of Socrates* (New York, 1992).

Brickhouse, T. C. and Smith, N. D., *Socrates on Trial* (Oxford, 1989).

Burnyeat, M. F., 'Socratic Midwifery, Platonic Inspiration', *Bulletin of the Institute of Classical Studies* 24 (1977), 7–16.

Ferrari, G. R. F., 'Plato and Poetry', in G. Kennedy, ed., *Cambridge History of Classical Literary Criticism*, vol. 1 (Cambridge, 1989), 92–148.

Fine, G., 'Inquiry in the *Meno*', in Kraut (1992), 200–226.

Gill, C., 'Plato on Falsehood – not Fiction', in Gill and Wiseman (1993), 38–87.

——'Afterword: Dialectic and the Dialogue Form in Late Plato', in Gill and McCabe (1996), 283–311.

Gill, C. and McCabe, M. M., eds, *Form and Argument in Late Plato* (Oxford, 1996).

Griswold, L., ed., *Platonic Writings, Platonic Readings* (New York, 1988).

Guthrie, W. K. C., *A History of Greek Philosophy*, vol. 3: *The Fifth-century Enlightenment* (Cambridge, 1969); vol. 4: *Plato, the Man and his Dialogues* (Cambridge, 1975).

Irwin, T., *Plato's Moral Theory* (Oxford, 1977).

——*Classical Thought* (Oxford, 1989), esp. 68–117.

—— *Plato's Ethics* (Oxford, 1995).

Janaway, C., *Images of Excellence: Plato's Critique of the Arts* (Oxford, 1995).

Kahn, C. H., 'Plato's Theory of Desire', *Review of Metaphysics* 41 (1987), 77–103.

——*Plato and the Socratic Dialogue: The Philosophical Use of a Literary Form* (Cambridge, 1996).

Klagge, J. C. and Smith, N. D., eds, *Methods of Interpreting Plato and his Dialogues*, *Oxford Studies in Ancient Philosophy*, supplementary volume (Oxford, 1992).

Kraut, R., ed., *The Cambridge Companion to Plato* (Cambridge, 1992).

Loizou, A. and Lesser, H., eds, *Polis and Politics: Essays in Greek Moral and Political Philosophy* (Aldershot, 1990).

Penner, T., 'Socrates and the Early Dialogues', in Kraut (1992), 121–69.

Price, A. W., 'Plato and Freud', in Gill (1990a), 247–70.

Rowe, C. J., 'Philosophy, Love and Madness', in Gill (1990a), 227–46.

Rutherford, R. B., *The Art of Plato* (London, 1995).

Vlastos, G., ed., *The Philosophy of Socrates: A Collection of Critical Essays*, vol. 2, *Ethics, Politics, and Philosophy of Art* (Garden City, NY, 1971).

——*Platonic Studies* (2nd edn, Princeton, 1981).

——*Socrates: Ironist and Moral Philosopher* (Cambridge, 1991).

——*Socratic Studies*, ed. M. F. Burnyeat (Cambridge, 1994).

Werkmeister, W. H., ed., *Facets of Plato's Philosophy* (Assen, 1976).

White, N. P., 'Plato's Metaphysical Epistemology', in Kraut (1992), 277–310.

For further bibliography on Socrates and Plato, see also these volumes of the journal *Lustrum*: 4 (1959), 5 (1960), 20 (1977), 25 (1983); and

McKirahan, R. D., *Plato and Socrates: A Comprehensive Bibliography 1958–73* (New York, 1978).

Katz, E. L. and Navia, L. E., *Socrates: An Annotated Biography* (London, 1988).

Kraut (1992), 493–529.

Related Topics

Allen, M. J. B., *The Platonism of Marsilio Ficino: A Study of his Phaedrus Commentary, its Source and Genesis* (Berkeley, 1984).

Bremmer, J. N., 'Adolescents, *Symposion* and Pederasty', in Murray (1990), 135–48.

Davidson, J., *Courtesans and Fishcakes* (London, 1997).

Dodds, E. R., *The Greeks and the Irrational* (Berkeley, 1951).

Dover, K. J., *Greek Homosexuality* (London, 1978).

Foucault, M., *The Uses of Pleasure: A History of Sexuality*, vol. 2, trans. R. Hurley (Harmondsworth, 1987).

Gill, C., ed., *The Person and the Human Mind: Issues in Ancient and Modern Philosophy* (Oxford, 1990a).

——'Altruism or Reciprocity in Greek Philosophy?', in Gill, Postlethwaite and Seaford (1998), 303–28.

Gill, C., Postlethwaite, N. and Seaford, R., eds, *Reciprocity in Ancient Greece* (Oxford, 1998).

Gill, C. and Wiseman, T. P., eds, *Lies and Fiction in the Ancient World* (Exeter, 1993).

Goldhill, S., *Foucault's Virginity: Ancient Erotic Fiction and the History of Sexuality* (Cambridge, 1995).

Halperin, D. M., *One Hundred Years of Homosexuality and Other Essays on Greek Love* (New York, 1990).

——'Homosexuality', in Hornblower and Spawforth (1996), 720–23.

Halperin, D. M., Winkler, J. J. and Zeitlin, F., eds, *Before Sexuality* (Princeton, 1990).

Hornblower, S. and Spawforth, A., eds, *The Oxford Classical Dictionary* (3rd edn, Oxford, 1996).

Jenkyns, R., *The Victorians and Ancient Greece* (Oxford, 1980).

Kahn, C. H., *The Art and Thought of Heraclitus* (Cambridge, 1979).

Konstan, D., *Sexual Symmetry: Love in the Ancient Novel and Related Genres* (Princeton, 1994).

——'Friendship and Reciprocity', in Gill, Postlethwaite and Seaford (1998), 279–301.

Kristeller, P. O., *The Philosophy of Marsilio Ficino*, trans. V. Conant (Gloucester, Mass., 1964).

Lacey, W. K., *The Family in Classical Greece* (London, 1968).

Lloyd, G. E. R., *Methods and Problems in Greek Science* (Cambridge, 1991).

Murray, O., ed., *Sympotica: A Symposium on the Symposion* (Oxford, 1990).

Murray, O. and Tecusan, M., eds, *In Vino Veritas* (London, 1995).

Parker, R., 'Reciprocity in Greek Religion', in Gill, Postlethwaite and Seaford (1998), 105–25.

Winkler, J. J., *The Constraints of Desire: The Anthropology of Sex and Gender in Ancient Greece* (New York, 1990).

Zanker, P., *The Mask of Socrates: The Image of the Intellectual in Antiquity*, trans. A. Shapiro (Berkeley, 1995).

READ MORE IN PENGUIN

A CHOICE OF CLASSICS

Aeschylus	**The Oresteian Trilogy**
	Prometheus Bound/The Suppliants/Seven against Thebes/The Persians
Aesop	**The Complete Fables**
Ammianus Marcellinus	**The Later Roman Empire (AD 354–378)**
Apollonius of Rhodes	**The Voyage of Argo**
Apuleius	**The Golden Ass**
Aristophanes	**The Knights/Peace/The Birds/The Assemblywomen/Wealth**
	Lysistrata/The Acharnians/The Clouds
	The Wasps/The Poet and the Women/ The Frogs
Aristotle	**The Art of Rhetoric**
	The Athenian Constitution
	Classic Literary Criticism
	De Anima
	The Metaphysics
	Ethics
	Poetics
	The Politics
Arrian	**The Campaigns of Alexander**
Marcus Aurelius	**Meditations**
Boethius	**The Consolation of Philosophy**
Caesar	**The Civil War**
	The Conquest of Gaul
Cicero	**Murder Trials**
	The Nature of the Gods
	On the Good Life
	On Government
	Selected Letters
	Selected Political Speeches
	Selected Works
Euripides	**Alcestis/Iphigenia in Tauris/Hippolytus**
	The Bacchae/Ion/The Women of Troy/ Helen
	Medea/Hecabe/Electra/Heracles
	Orestes and Other Plays

READ MORE IN PENGUIN

A CHOICE OF CLASSICS

Hesiod/Theognis	**Theogony/Works and Days/Elegies**
Hippocrates	**Hippocratic Writings**
Homer	**The Iliad**
	The Odyssey
Horace	**Complete Odes and Epodes**
Horace/Persius	**Satires and Epistles**
Juvenal	**The Sixteen Satires**
Livy	**The Early History of Rome**
	Rome and Italy
	Rome and the Mediterranean
	The War with Hannibal
Lucretius	**On the Nature of the Universe**
Martial	**Epigrams**
	Martial in English
Ovid	**The Erotic Poems**
	Heroides
	Metamorphoses
	The Poems of Exile
Pausanias	**Guide to Greece (In two volumes)**
Petronius/Seneca	**The Satyricon/The Apocolocyntosis**
Pindar	**The Odes**
Plato	**Early Socratic Dialogues**
	Gorgias
	The Last Days of Socrates (Euthyphro/ The Apology/Crito/Phaedo)
	The Laws
	Phaedrus and Letters VII and VIII
	Philebus
	Protagoras/Meno
	The Republic
	The Symposium
	Theaetetus
	Timaeus/Critias
Plautus	**The Pot of Gold and Other Plays**
	The Rope and Other Plays

READ MORE IN PENGUIN

A CHOICE OF CLASSICS

Pliny	**The Letters of the Younger Pliny**
Pliny the Elder	**Natural History**
Plotinus	**The Enneads**
Plutarch	**The Age of Alexander (Nine Greek Lives)**
	Essays
	The Fall of the Roman Republic (Six Lives)
	The Makers of Rome (Nine Lives)
	Plutarch on Sparta
	The Rise and Fall of Athens (Nine Greek Lives)
Polybius	**The Rise of the Roman Empire**
Procopius	**The Secret History**
Propertius	**The Poems**
Quintus Curtius Rufus	**The History of Alexander**
Sallust	**The Jugurthine War/The Conspiracy of Cataline**
Seneca	**Dialogues and Letters**
	Four Tragedies/Octavia
	Letters from a Stoic
	Seneca in English
Sophocles	**Electra/Women of Trachis/Philoctetes/Ajax**
	The Theban Plays
Suetonius	**The Twelve Caesars**
Tacitus	**The Agricola/The Germania**
	The Annals of Imperial Rome
	The Histories
Terence	**The Comedies (The Girl from Andros/The Self-Tormentor/The Eunuch/Phormio/ The Mother-in-Law/The Brothers)**
Thucydides	**History of the Peloponnesian War**
Virgil	**The Aeneid**
	The Eclogues
	The Georgics
Xenophon	**Conversations of Socrates**
	Hiero the Tyrant
	A History of My Times
	The Persian Expedition

THE STORY OF PENGUIN CLASSICS

Before 1946 ...'Classics' are mainly the domain of academics and students, without readable editions for everyone else. This all changes when a little-known classicist, E. V. Rieu, presents Penguin founder Allen Lane with the translation of Homer's *Odyssey* that he has been working on and reading to his wife Nelly in his spare time.

1946 *The Odyssey* becomes the first Penguin Classic published, and promptly sells three million copies. Suddenly, classic books are no longer for the privileged few.

1950s Rieu, now series editor, turns to professional writers for the best modern, readable translations, including Dorothy L. Sayers's *Inferno* and Robert Graves's *The Twelve Caesars*, which revives the salacious original.

1960s The Classics are given the distinctive black jackets that have remained a constant throughout the series's various looks. Rieu retires in 1964, hailing the Penguin Classics list as 'the greatest educative force of the 20th century'.

1970s A new generation of translators arrives to swell the Penguin Classics ranks, and the list grows to encompass more philosophy, religion, science, history and politics.

1980s The Penguin American Library joins the Classics stable, with titles such as *The Last of the Mohicans* safeguarded. Penguin Classics now offers the most comprehensive library of world literature available.

1990s The launch of Penguin Audiobooks brings the classics to a listening audience for the first time, and in 1999 the launch of the Penguin Classics website takes them online to a larger global readership than ever before.

The 21st Century Penguin Classics are rejacketed for the first time in nearly twenty years. This world famous series now consists of more than 1300 titles, making the widest range of the best books ever written available to millions – and constantly redefining the meaning of what makes a 'classic'.

The Odyssey continues ...

The best books ever written

PENGUIN 🐧 CLASSICS

SINCE 1946

Find out more at www.penguinclassics.com